EAGLE® BRAND

CLASSIC RECIPES™

Publications International, Ltd.
Favorite Brand Name Recipes at www.fbnr.com

Microwave Cooking: Microwave ovens vary in wattage. Use the cooking times as
guidelines and check for doneness before adding more time.

Preparation/Cooking Times: Preparation times are based on the approximate amount
of time required to assemble the recipe before cooking, baking, chilling or serving. These
times include preparation steps such as measuring, chopping and mixing. The fact that
some preparations and cooking can be done simultaneously is taken into account.
Preparation of optional ingredients and serving suggestions is not included.

Table of Contents

Fabulous Bars 6

Sensational Cookies 36

Luscious Cakes & Cheesecakes . . .50

Glorious Pies 74

Creamy Candy & Desserts 94

Index .123

Fabulous Bars

Who can resist Magic Cookie Bars? No one can! This is just one of the Eagle® Brand classics that has been loved by families for generations.

Magic Cookie Bars

$^1/_2$ cup (1 stick) butter or margarine
1$^1/_2$ cups graham cracker crumbs
1 (14-ounce) can EAGLE® BRAND Sweetened Condensed Milk
   (NOT evaporated milk)
2 cups (12 ounces) semi-sweet chocolate chips
1$^1/_3$ cups flaked coconut
1 cup chopped nuts

1. Preheat oven to 350°F (325°F for glass dish). In 13×9-inch baking pan, melt butter in oven.

2. Sprinkle crumbs over butter; pour Eagle Brand evenly over crumbs. Layer evenly with remaining ingredients; press down firmly.

3. Bake 25 minutes or until lightly browned. Cool. Chill, if desired. Cut into bars. Store loosely covered at room temperature.

Makes 2 to 3 dozen bars

Prep Time: 10 minutes
Bake Time: 25 minutes

7-Layer Magic Cookie Bars: Substitute 1 cup (6 ounces) butterscotch-flavored chips* for 1 cup semi-sweet chocolate chips.

* Peanut butter-flavored chips or white chips may be substituted for butterscotch-flavored chips.

Magic Peanut Cookie Bars: Substitute 2 cups (about $^3/_4$ pound) chocolate-covered peanuts for semi-sweet chocolate chips and chopped nuts.

Magic Rainbow Cookie Bars: Substitute 2 cups plain candy-coated chocolate pieces for semi-sweet chocolate chips.

Double Chocolate Fantasy Bars

    1 (18.25-ounce) package chocolate cake mix
  ¼ cup vegetable oil
    1 egg
    1 cup chopped nuts
    1 (14-ounce) can EAGLE® BRAND Sweetened Condensed Milk
       (NOT evaporated milk)
    1 (6-ounce) package semi-sweet chocolate chips
    1 teaspoon vanilla extract
      Dash salt

1. Preheat oven to 350°F. Grease 13×9-inch baking pan. In large mixing bowl, combine cake mix, oil and egg; beat at medium speed until crumbly. Stir in nuts. Reserve 1½ cups crumb mixture. Press remaining crumb mixture on bottom of prepared pan.

2. In small saucepan over medium heat, combine remaining ingredients. Cook and stir until chips melt.

3. Pour chocolate mixture evenly over prepared crust. Sprinkle reserved crumb mixture evenly over top. Bake 25 to 30 minutes or until set. Cool. Cut into bars. Store loosely covered at room temperature.

Makes about 3 dozen bars

Prep Time: 15 minutes
Bake Time: 25 to 30 minutes

Top to bottom: Double Chocolate Fantasy Bars and Toffee Bars (page 19)

Chewy Almond Squares

1 1/4 cups graham cracker crumbs
1/3 cup (2/3 stick) butter or margarine, melted
1/4 cup sugar
1 cup flaked coconut, toasted
1 cup chopped almonds, toasted*
1 (14-ounce) can EAGLE® BRAND Sweetened Condensed Milk
(NOT evaporated milk)

*1 cup chopped pecans or walnuts, toasted, may be substituted.

1. Preheat oven to 375°F. Line 9-inch square pan with foil. In medium mixing bowl, combine crumbs, butter and sugar. Press into bottom of prepared pan. Bake 5 to 7 minutes.

2. Sprinkle crust with coconut and almonds; pour Eagle Brand evenly over surface.

3. Bake 25 to 30 minutes. Cool on wire rack. Cut into squares. Store covered at room temperature.   *Makes 16 squares*

Prep Time: 10 minutes
Bake Time: 30 to 37 minutes

Top to bottom: Chewy Almond Squares and Marbled Cheesecake Bars (page 12)

Marbled Cheesecake Bars

2 cups finely crushed crème-filled chocolate sandwich cookie
    crumbs (about 24 cookies)

3 tablespoons butter or margarine, melted

3 (8-ounce) packages cream cheese, softened

1 (14-ounce) can EAGLE® BRAND Sweetened Condensed Milk
    (NOT evaporated milk)

3 eggs

2 teaspoons vanilla extract

2 (1-ounce) squares unsweetened chocolate, melted

1. Preheat oven to 300°F. Line 13×9-inch baking pan with heavy foil; set aside. Combine crumbs and butter; press firmly on bottom of prepared pan.

2. In large mixing bowl, beat cream cheese until fluffy. Gradually beat in Eagle Brand until smooth. Add eggs and vanilla; mix well. Pour half the batter evenly over prepared crust.

3. Stir melted chocolate into remaining batter; spoon over vanilla batter. With table knife or metal spatula, gently swirl through batter to marble.

4. Bake 45 to 50 minutes or until set. Cool. Chill. Cut into bars. Store covered in refrigerator.   *Makes 2 to 3 dozen bars*

Prep Time: 20 minutes
Bake Time: 45 to 50 minutes

Helpful Hint: For even marbling, do not oversoften or overbeat the cream cheese.

Brownie Mint Sundae Squares

1 (21.5- or 23.6-ounce) package fudge brownie mix
$^3/_4$ cup coarsely chopped walnuts
1 (14-ounce) can EAGLE® BRAND Sweetened Condensed Milk
(NOT evaporated milk)
2 teaspoons peppermint extract
Green food coloring, if desired
2 cups (1 pint) whipping cream, whipped
$^1/_2$ cup mini chocolate chips
Chocolate ice cream topping, if desired

1. Line 13×9-inch baking pan with aluminum foil; grease foil. Prepare brownie mix as package directs; stir in walnuts. Spread in prepared pan. Bake as directed. Cool completely.

2. In large mixing bowl, combine Eagle Brand, peppermint extract and food coloring, if desired. Fold in whipped cream and chips. Pour over brownie layer; cover.

3. Freeze 6 hours or until firm. To serve, lift brownies from pan with foil; cut into squares. Serve with chocolate ice cream topping, if desired. Freeze leftovers. *Makes 12 servings*

Cheesecake-Topped Brownies

1 (21.5- or 23.6-ounce) package fudge brownie mix
1 (8-ounce) package cream cheese, softened
2 tablespoons butter or margarine, softened
1 tablespoon cornstarch
1 (14-ounce) can EAGLE® BRAND Sweetened Condensed Milk
(NOT evaporated milk)
1 egg
2 teaspoons vanilla extract
Ready-to-spread chocolate frosting, if desired
Orange peel, if desired

1. Preheat oven to 350°F. Prepare brownie mix as package directs. Spread into well-greased 13×9-inch baking pan.

2. In large mixing bowl, beat cream cheese, butter and cornstarch until fluffy.

3. Gradually beat in Eagle Brand. Add egg and vanilla; beat until smooth. Pour cheesecake mixture evenly over brownie batter.

4. Bake 40 to 45 minutes or until top is lightly browned. Cool. Spread with frosting or sprinkle with orange peel, if desired. Cut into bars. Store covered in refrigerator.   *Makes 3 to 3½ dozen brownies*

Prep Time: 20 minutes
Bake Time: 40 to 45 minutes

Cheesecake-Topped Brownies

Chocolate Nut Bars

1 3/4 cups graham cracker crumbs

1/2 cup (1 stick) butter or margarine, melted

1 (14-ounce) can EAGLE® BRAND Sweetened Condensed Milk
(NOT evaporated milk)

2 cups (12 ounces) semi-sweet chocolate chips, divided

1 teaspoon vanilla extract

1 cup chopped nuts

1. Preheat oven to 375°F. Combine crumbs and butter; press firmly on bottom of 13×9-inch baking pan. Bake 8 minutes. Reduce oven temperature to 350°F.

2. In small saucepan over medium heat, melt Eagle Brand with 1 cup chocolate chips and vanilla. Spread chocolate mixture over prepared crust. Top with remaining 1 cup chocolate chips, then nuts; press down firmly.

3. Bake 25 to 30 minutes. Cool. Chill if desired. Cut into bars. Store loosely covered at room temperature.   *Makes 2 to 3 dozen bars*

Prep Time: 10 minutes
Bake Time: 33 to 38 minutes

Chocolate Nut Bars

Lemony Cheesecake Bars

1 1/2 cups graham cracker crumbs

1/3 cup sugar

1/3 cup finely chopped pecans

1/3 cup butter or margarine, melted

2 (8-ounce) packages cream cheese, softened

1 (14-ounce) can EAGLE® BRAND Sweetened Condensed Milk (NOT evaporated milk)

2 eggs

1/2 cup lemon juice from concentrate

1. Preheat oven to 325°F. In medium mixing bowl, combine crumbs, sugar, pecans and melted butter. Reserve 1/3 cup crumb mixture; press remaining mixture into 13×9-inch baking pan. Bake 5 minutes. Remove from oven and cool on wire rack.

2. In large mixing bowl, beat cream cheese until fluffy. Gradually beat in Eagle Brand until smooth. Add eggs; beat until just combined. Stir in lemon juice. Carefully spoon mixture onto crust in pan. Spoon reserved crumb mixture to make diagonal stripes on top of cheese mixture or sprinkle to cover.

3. Bake about 30 minutes or until knife inserted near center comes out clean. Cool on wire rack 1 hour. Cut into bars to serve. Store in refrigerator. *Makes 3 dozen bars*

Prep Time: 25 minutes
Bake Time: 35 minutes

Toffee Bars

1 cup quick-cooking oats
$^1/_2$ cup all-purpose flour
$^1/_2$ cup firmly packed light brown sugar
$^1/_2$ cup finely chopped walnuts
$^1/_2$ cup (1 stick) butter or margarine, melted and divided
$^1/_4$ teaspoon baking soda
1 (14-ounce) can EAGLE® BRAND Sweetened Condensed Milk
    (NOT evaporated milk)
2 teaspoons vanilla extract
2 cups (12 ounces) semi-sweet chocolate chips
Additional chopped walnuts, if desired

1. Preheat oven to 350°F. Grease 13×9-inch baking pan. In large mixing bowl, combine oats, flour, brown sugar, walnuts, 6 tablespoons butter and baking soda. Press firmly on bottom of prepared pan. Bake 10 to 15 minutes or until lightly browned.

2. Meanwhile, in medium saucepan over medium heat, combine remaining 2 tablespoons butter and Eagle Brand. Cook and stir until mixture thickens slightly, about 15 minutes. Remove from heat; stir in vanilla. Pour evenly over baked crust.

3. Bake 10 to 15 minutes or until golden brown.

4. Remove from oven; immediately sprinkle chips on top. Let stand 1 minute; spread chips while still warm. Garnish with additional walnuts, if desired; press down firmly. Cool completely. Cut into bars. Store tightly covered at room temperature. *Makes 3 dozen bars*

Lemon Crumb Bars

1 (18.25-ounce) package lemon or yellow cake mix

$^1/_2$ cup (1 stick) butter or margarine, softened

1 egg

2 cups finely crushed saltine cracker crumbs

3 egg yolks

1 (14-ounce) can EAGLE® BRAND Sweetened Condensed Milk
(NOT evaporated milk)

$^1/_2$ cup lemon juice from concentrate

1. Preheat oven to 350°F. Grease 15×10-inch jelly-roll pan. In large mixing bowl, combine cake mix, butter and 1 egg; mix well (mixture will be crumbly). Stir in cracker crumbs. Reserve 2 cups crumb mixture. Press remaining crumb mixture firmly on bottom of prepared pan. Bake 15 minutes.

2. Meanwhile, in medium mixing bowl, combine egg yolks, Eagle Brand and lemon juice; mix well. Spread evenly over baked crust.

3. Top with reserved crumb mixture. Bake 20 minutes or until firm. Cool. Cut into bars. Store covered in refrigerator.   *Makes 3 to 4 dozen bars*

Prep Time: 30 minutes
Bake Time: 35 minutes

Lemon Crumb Bars

Toffee-Top Cheesecake Bars

1¼ cups all-purpose flour
1 cup powdered sugar
½ cup unsweetened cocoa
¼ teaspoon baking soda
¾ cup (1½ sticks) butter or margarine
1 (8-ounce) package cream cheese, softened
1 (14-ounce) can EAGLE® BRAND Sweetened Condensed Milk
    (NOT evaporated milk)
2 eggs
1 teaspoon vanilla extract
1½ cups (8-ounce package) English toffee bits, divided

1. Preheat oven 350°F. In medium mixing bowl, combine flour, powdered sugar, cocoa and baking soda; cut in butter until mixture is crumbly. Press into bottom of ungreased 13×9-inch baking pan. Bake 15 minutes.

2. Beat cream cheese until fluffy. Add Eagle Brand, eggs and vanilla; beat until smooth. Stir in 1 cup English toffee bits. Pour mixture over hot crust. Bake 25 minutes or until set and edges just begin to brown.

3. Remove from oven. Cool 15 minutes. Sprinkle remaining ½ cup English toffee bits evenly over top. Cool completely. Refrigerate several hours or until cold. Store leftovers covered in refrigerator.

Makes about 3 dozen bars

Prep Time: 20 minutes
Bake Time: 40 minutes
Cool Time: 15 minutes

Toffee-Top Cheesecake Bars

German Chocolate Cheesecake Bars

1½ cups graham cracker crumbs

½ cup sugar

½ cup butter or margarine, melted

3 (8-ounce) packages cream cheese, softened

1 (14-ounce) can EAGLE® BRAND Sweetened Condensed Milk
    (NOT evaporated milk)

2 (4-ounce) packages semi-sweet chocolate, melted

3 eggs

1 tablespoon vanilla extract

    Coconut Pecan Topping (recipe follows)

1. Preheat oven to 350°F. In medium mixing bowl, combine crumbs, sugar and butter; press on bottom of 15×10-inch jelly-roll pan. In large mixing bowl, beat cream cheese until fluffy. Gradually beat in Eagle Brand until smooth. Add remaining ingredients except topping; mix well. Pour over crust.

2. Bake 20 minutes or until center is set. Cool. Top with Coconut Pecan Topping. Chill. Cut into bars. Refrigerate leftovers.

Makes 3 to 4 dozen bars

Coconut Pecan Topping

1 (14-ounce) can EAGLE® BRAND Sweetened Condensed Milk
    (NOT evaporated milk)

3 egg yolks

½ cup butter or margarine

1⅓ cups flaked coconut

1 cup chopped pecans

1 teaspoon vanilla extract

1. In heavy saucepan, combine Eagle Brand and egg yolks; mix well. Add butter. Over medium-low heat, cook and stir until thickened and bubbly, 8 to 10 minutes.

2. Remove saucepan from heat; stir in coconut, pecans and vanilla. Cool 10 minutes.   *Makes about 2³/₄ cups*

Frozen Lemon Squares

1¹/₄ cups graham cracker crumbs
 ¹/₄ cup sugar
 ¹/₄ cup (¹/₂ stick) butter or margarine, melted
  1 (14-ounce) can EAGLE® BRAND Sweetened Condensed Milk
     (NOT evaporated milk)
  3 egg yolks
 ¹/₂ cup lemon juice from concentrate
     Yellow food coloring, if desired
     Whipped cream or non-dairy whipped topping

1. Preheat oven to 325°F. Combine crumbs, sugar and butter; press firmly on bottom of 8- or 9-inch square pan.

2. In medium mixing bowl, beat Eagle Brand, egg yolks, lemon juice and food coloring, if desired. Pour into crust.

3. Bake 30 minutes. Cool completely. Top with whipped cream. Freeze 4 hours or until firm. Let stand 10 minutes before serving. Garnish as desired. Freeze leftovers.   *Makes 6 to 9 squares*

Fudge-Filled Bars

1 (14-ounce) can EAGLE® BRAND Sweetened Condensed Milk
(NOT evaporated milk)
1 (12-ounce) package semi-sweet chocolate chips
2 tablespoons butter or margarine
2 teaspoons vanilla extract
2 (18-ounce) packages refrigerated cookie dough (oatmeal-
chocolate chip, chocolate chip, or sugar cookie dough),
divided

1. Preheat oven to 350°F. In heavy saucepan over medium heat, combine
Eagle Brand, chips and butter; heat until chips melt, stirring often.
Remove from heat; stir in vanilla. Cool 15 minutes.

2. Using floured hands, press 1 1/2 packages of cookie dough into
ungreased 15×10-inch jelly-roll pan. Pour cooled chocolate mixture
evenly over dough. Crumble remaining dough over chocolate mixture.

3. Bake 25 to 30 minutes. Cool. Cut into bars. Store covered at room
temperature.   *Makes 4 dozen bars*

Prep Time: 20 minutes
Bake Time: 25 to 30 minutes

Helpful Hint: If you want to trim the fat in any Eagle Brand recipe, just
use Eagle® Brand Fat Free or Low Fat Sweetened Condensed Milk instead
of the original Eagle Brand.

Fudge-Filled Bars

No-Bake Fudgy Brownies

1 (14-ounce) can EAGLE® BRAND Sweetened Condensed Milk
   (NOT evaporated milk)
2 (1-ounce) squares unsweetened chocolate, cut up
1 teaspoon vanilla extract
2 cups plus 2 tablespoons packaged chocolate cookie crumbs,
   divided
1/4 cup miniature candy-coated milk chocolate candies or chopped
   nuts

1. Grease 8-inch square baking pan or line with foil; set aside.

2. In medium-sized heavy saucepan, combine Eagle Brand and chocolate;
cook and stir over low heat just until boiling. Reduce heat; cook and stir
for 2 to 3 minutes more or until mixture thickens. Remove from heat.
Stir in vanilla.

3. Stir in 2 cups cookie crumbs. Spread evenly in prepared pan. Sprinkle
with remaining cookie crumbs and candies or nuts; press down gently with
back of spoon.

4. Cover and chill 4 hours or until firm. Cut into squares. Store covered
in refrigerator.   *Makes 2 to 3 dozen brownies*

Prep Time: 10 minutes
Chill Time: 4 hours

No-Bake Fudgy Brownies

Buckeye Cookie Bars

1 (18.25-ounce) package chocolate cake mix
¹/₄ cup vegetable oil
1 egg
1 cup chopped peanuts
1 (14-ounce) can EAGLE® BRAND Sweetened Condensed Milk
    (NOT evaporated milk)
¹/₂ cup peanut butter

1. Preheat oven to 350°F. In large mixing bowl, combine cake mix, oil and egg; beat at medium speed until crumbly. Stir in peanuts. Reserve 1¹/₂ cups crumb mixture; press remaining crumb mixture firmly on bottom of greased 13×9 inch baking pan.

2. In medium mixing bowl, beat Eagle Brand with peanut butter until smooth; spread over prepared crust. Sprinkle with reserved crumb mixture.

3. Bake 25 to 30 minutes or until set. Cool. Cut into bars. Store loosely covered at room temperature. *Makes 2 to 3 dozen bars*

Prep Time: 20 minutes
Bake Time: 25 to 30 minutes

Double Chocolate Brownies

1 1/4 cups all-purpose flour, divided

1/4 cup sugar

1/2 cup (1 stick) cold butter or margarine

1 (14-ounce) can EAGLE® BRAND Sweetened Condensed Milk
     (NOT evaporated milk)

1/4 cup unsweetened cocoa

1 egg

1 teaspoon vanilla extract

1/2 teaspoon baking powder

1 (8-ounce) milk chocolate bar, broken into chunks

3/4 cup chopped nuts, if desired

1. Preheat oven to 350°F. Line 13×9-inch baking pan with foil; set aside.

2. In medium mixing bowl, combine 1 cup flour and sugar; cut in butter until crumbly. Press firmly on bottom of prepared pan. Bake 15 minutes.

3. In large mixing bowl, beat Eagle Brand, cocoa, egg, remaining 1/4 cup flour, vanilla and baking powder. Stir in chocolate chunks and nuts, if desired. Spread over baked crust. Bake 20 minutes or until set.

4. Cool. Use foil to lift out of pan. Cut into bars. Store tightly covered at room temperature.   *Makes 2 dozen brownies*

Prep Time: 15 minutes
Bake Time: 35 minutes

Double Delicious Cookie Bars

$^1/_2$ cup (1 stick) butter or margarine

$1^1/_2$ cups graham cracker crumbs

1 (14-ounce) can EAGLE® BRAND Sweetened Condensed Milk
   (NOT evaporated milk)

2 cups (12 ounces) semi-sweet chocolate chips*

1 cup (6 ounces) peanut butter-flavored chips*

Butterscotch-flavored chips or white chocolate chips can be substituted for the semi-sweet chocolate chips and/or peanut butter-flavored chips.

1. Preheat oven to 350°F (325°F for glass dish). In 13×9-inch baking pan, melt butter in oven.

2. Sprinkle crumbs evenly over butter; pour Eagle Brand evenly over crumbs. Top with remaining ingredients; press down firmly.

3. Bake 25 to 30 minutes or until lightly browned. Cool. Cut into bars. Store covered at room temperature.   *Makes 2 to 3 dozen bars*

Prep Time: 10 minutes
Bake Time: 25 to 30 minutes

Double Delicious Cookie Bars

Golden Peanut Butter Bars

2 cups all-purpose flour

3/4 cup firmly packed light brown sugar

1 egg, beaten

1/2 cup (1 stick) cold butter or margarine

1 cup finely chopped peanuts

1 (14-ounce) can EAGLE® BRAND Sweetened Condensed Milk
(NOT evaporated milk)

1/2 cup peanut butter

1 teaspoon vanilla extract

1. Preheat oven to 350°F. In large mixing bowl, combine flour, brown sugar and egg; cut in cold butter until crumbly. Stir in peanuts. Reserve 2 cups crumb mixture. Press remaining mixture on bottom of 13×9-inch baking pan.

2. Bake 15 minutes or until lightly browned.

3. Meanwhile, in another large mixing bowl, beat Eagle Brand, peanut butter and vanilla. Spread over prepared crust; top with reserved crumb mixture.

4. Bake an additional 25 minutes or until lightly browned. Cool. Cut into bars. Store covered at room temperature.   *Makes 2 to 3 dozen bars*

Prep Time: 20 minutes
Bake Time: 40 minutes

Golden Peanut Butter Bars

Sensational Cookies

Fill your cookie jar with scrumptious treats. You can whip up these cookies in minutes and watch them disappear quicker than a wink!

Chocolate Peanut Butter Chip Cookies

8 (1-ounce) squares semi-sweet chocolate

3 tablespoons butter or margarine

1 (14-ounce) can EAGLE® BRAND Sweetened Condensed Milk
    (NOT evaporated milk)

2 cups biscuit baking mix

1 egg

1 teaspoon vanilla extract

1 cup (6 ounces) peanut butter-flavored chips

1. Preheat oven to 350°F. In large saucepan over low heat, melt chocolate and butter with Eagle Brand; remove from heat. Add biscuit mix, egg and vanilla; with mixer, beat until smooth and well blended.

2. Let mixture cool to room temperature. Stir in peanut butter chips. Shape into 1¼-inch balls. Place 2 inches apart on ungreased baking sheets. Bake 6 to 8 minutes or until tops are lightly crusty. Cool. Store tightly covered at room temperature.   *Makes about 4 dozen cookies*

Prep Time: 15 minutes
Bake Time: 6 to 8 minutes

Double Chocolate Cherry Cookies

1¼ cups (2½ sticks) butter or margarine, softened

1¾ cups sugar

2 eggs

1 tablespoon vanilla extract

3½ cups all-purpose flour

¾ cup unsweetened cocoa

½ teaspoon baking powder

½ teaspoon baking soda

¼ teaspoon salt

2 (6-ounce) jars maraschino cherries, well drained and halved (about 60 cherries)

1 (6-ounce) package semi-sweet chocolate chips

1 (14-ounce) can EAGLE® BRAND Sweetened Condensed Milk (NOT evaporated milk)

1. Preheat oven to 350°F. In large mixing bowl, beat butter and sugar until fluffy. Add eggs and vanilla; mix well.

2. In large mixing bowl, combine dry ingredients; stir into butter mixture (dough will be stiff). Shape into 1-inch balls. Place 1 inch apart on ungreased baking sheets. Press cherry half into center of each cookie. Bake 8 to 10 minutes. Cool.

3. In heavy saucepan over medium heat, melt chips with Eagle Brand; cook until mixture thickens, about 3 minutes. Frost each cookie, covering cherry. Store loosely covered at room temperature.

Makes about 10 dozen cookies

Prep Time: 25 minutes
Bake Time: 8 to 10 minutes

Double Chocolate Pecan Cookies: Prepare and shape dough as directed above, omitting cherries. Flatten. Bake and frost as directed. Garnish each cookie with pecan half.

Coconut Macaroons

> 1 (14-ounce) can EAGLE® BRAND Sweetened Condensed Milk (NOT evaporated milk)
> 2 teaspoons vanilla extract
> 1 to 1 1/2 teaspoons almond extract
> 2 (7-ounce) packages flaked coconut (5 1/3 cups)

1. Preheat oven to 325°F. Line baking sheets with foil; grease and flour foil. Set aside.

2. In large mixing bowl, combine Eagle Brand, vanilla and almond extract. Stir in coconut. Drop by rounded teaspoonfuls onto prepared sheets; with spoon, slightly flatten each mound.

3. Bake 15 to 17 minutes or until golden. Remove from baking sheets; cool on wire racks. Store loosely covered at room temperature.

Makes about 4 dozen cookies

Prep Time: 10 minutes
Bake Time: 15 to 17 minutes

Chocolate Chip Treasure Cookies

1 1/2 cups graham cracker crumbs

1/2 cup all-purpose flour

2 teaspoons baking powder

1 (14-ounce) can EAGLE® BRAND Sweetened Condensed Milk
(NOT evaporated milk)

1/2 cup (1 stick) butter or margarine, softened

1 1/3 cups flaked coconut

1 (12-ounce) package semi-sweet chocolate chips

1 cup chopped walnuts

1. Preheat oven to 375°F. In small mixing bowl, combine crumbs, flour and baking powder.

2. In large mixing bowl, beat Eagle Brand and butter until smooth. Add crumb mixture; mix well. Stir in coconut, chips and walnuts.

3. Drop by rounded tablespoonfuls onto ungreased cookie sheets. Bake 9 to 10 minutes or until lightly browned. Store loosely covered at room temperature.   *Makes about 3 dozen cookies*

Prep Time: 15 minutes
Bake Time: 9 to 10 minutes

Clockwise from top: Chocolate Chip Treasure Cookies, Cookies 'n' Crème Fudge (page 114), Double Chocolate Brownie (page 31) and Magic Cookie Bar (page 7)

Magic Make It Your Way Drop Cookies

    3 cups sifted all-purpose flour
    3 teaspoons baking powder
  3/4 teaspoon salt
  3/4 cup (1 1/2 sticks) butter or margarine, softened
    2 eggs
    1 teaspoon vanilla extract
    1 (14-ounce) can EAGLE® BRAND Sweetened Condensed Milk
        (NOT evaporated milk)
    One "favorite" ingredient (see below)

1. Preheat oven to 350°F. Grease baking sheets; set aside. In large mixing bowl, sift together dry ingredients. Stir in butter, eggs, vanilla and Eagle Brand. Fold in one of your "favorite" ingredients.

2. Drop by level teaspoonfuls, about 2 inches apart, onto prepared baking sheets. Bake 8 to 10 minutes or until edges are slightly browned. Remove at once from baking sheet. Cool. Store covered at room temperature.

Makes about 4 dozen cookies

"Make it your way" with your favorite ingredient (pick one):
1 (6-ounce) package semi-sweet chocolate chips
1 1/2 cups raisins
1 1/2 cups corn flakes
1 1/2 cups toasted shredded coconut

Prep Time: 15 minutes
Bake Time: 8 to 10 minutes

No-Bake Peanutty Chocolate Drops

$1/2$ cup (1 stick) butter or margarine

$1/3$ cup unsweetened cocoa

$2^1/2$ cups quick-cooking oats

1 (14-ounce) can EAGLE® BRAND Sweetened Condensed Milk
(NOT evaporated milk)

1 cup chopped peanuts

$1/2$ cup peanut butter

1. Line baking sheets with waxed paper. In medium saucepan over medium heat, melt butter; stir in cocoa. Bring mixture to a boil.

2. Remove from heat; stir in remaining ingredients.

3. Drop by teaspoonfuls onto prepared baking sheets; chill 2 hours or until set. Store loosely covered in refrigerator.

Makes about 5 dozen drops

Prep Time: 10 minutes
Chill Time: 2 hours

Double Chocolate Cookies

2 cups biscuit baking mix

1 (14-ounce) can EAGLE® BRAND Sweetened Condensed Milk (NOT evaporated milk)

8 (1-ounce) squares semi-sweet chocolate *or* 1 (12-ounce) package semi-sweet chocolate chips, melted

3 tablespoons butter or margarine, melted

1 egg

1 teaspoon vanilla extract

6 (1 1/4-ounce) white chocolate candy bars with almonds, broken into small pieces

3/4 cup chopped nuts

1. Preheat oven to 350°F. In large mixing bowl, combine all ingredients except candy pieces and nuts; beat until smooth.

2. Stir in remaining ingredients. Drop by rounded teaspoonfuls, 2 inches apart, onto ungreased baking sheets.

3. Bake 10 minutes or until tops are slightly crusted (do not overbake). Cool. Store tightly covered at room temperature.

Makes about 4 1/2 dozen cookies

Prep Time: 15 minutes
Bake Time: 10 minutes

Mint Chocolate Cookies: Substitute 3/4 cup mint-flavored chocolate chips for white chocolate candy bars with almonds. Proceed as directed above.

Top to bottom: Double Chocolate Cookies and Chocolate Raspberry Truffles (page 08)

Macaroon Kisses

1 (14-ounce) can EAGLE® BRAND Sweetened Condensed Milk
  (NOT evaporated milk)
2 teaspoons vanilla extract
1 to 1$^1/_2$ teaspoons almond extract
5$^1/_3$ cups (14 ounces) flaked coconut
48 solid milk chocolate candy kisses, stars or drops, unwrapped

1. Preheat oven to 325°F. Line baking sheets with foil; grease and flour foil. Set aside.

2. In large mixing bowl, combine Eagle Brand, vanilla and almond extract. Stir in coconut. Drop by rounded teaspoonfuls onto foil-lined sheets; slightly flatten each mound with spoon.

3. Bake 15 to 17 minutes or until golden brown. Remove from oven. Immediately press candy kiss, star or drop in center of each macaroon. Remove from baking sheets; cool on wire racks. Store loosely covered at room temperature.   *Makes 4 dozen cookies*

To measure Eagle Brand easily, remove the entire lid first, and then scrape the Eagle Brand into a glass measuring cup using a rubber scraper.

Macaroon Kisses

Easy Peanut Butter Cookies

1 (14-ounce) can EAGLE® BRAND Sweetened Condensed Milk
(NOT evaporated milk)
3/4 to 1 cup peanut butter
1 egg
1 teaspoon vanilla extract
2 cups biscuit baking mix
Sugar

1. In large mixing bowl, beat Eagle Brand, peanut butter, egg and vanilla until smooth. Add biscuit mix; mix well. Chill at least 1 hour.

2. Preheat oven to 350°F. Shape dough into 1-inch balls. Roll in sugar. Place 2 inches apart on ungreased baking sheets.

3. Flatten with fork in criss-cross pattern. Bake 6 to 8 minutes or until lightly browned (do not overbake). Cool. Store tightly covered at room temperature.   *Makes about 5 dozen cookies*

Prep Time: 10 minutes
Chill Time: 1 hour
Bake Time: 6 to 8 minutes

Peanut Butter & Jelly Gems: Make dough as directed above. Shape into 1-inch balls and roll in sugar; do not flatten. Press thumb in center of each ball of dough; fill with jelly, jam or preserves. Proceed as directed above.

Any-Way-You-Like 'em Cookies: Stir 1 cup semi-sweet chocolate chips, chopped peanuts, raisins or flaked coconut into dough. Proceed as directed above.

Peanut Blossom Cookies

1 (14-ounce) can EAGLE® BRAND Sweetened Condensed Milk
  (NOT evaporated milk)
$^3/_4$ cup peanut butter
2 cups biscuit mix
1 teaspoon vanilla extract
$^1/_3$ cup sugar
60 solid milk chocolate candy kisses, unwrapped

1. Preheat oven to 375°F. In large mixing bowl, beat Eagle Brand and peanut butter until smooth. Add biscuit mix and vanilla; mix well. Shape into 1-inch balls. Roll in sugar. Place 2-inches apart on ungreased baking sheets.

2. Bake 6 to 8 minutes or until lightly browned (do not overbake). Immediately remove from oven; press candy kiss in center of each cookie. Cool. Store tightly covered at room temperature.

Makes about 5 dozen cookies

Cookies and desserts made with Eagle Brand contain condensed all-natural milk. This gives your family important bone-building calcium in every bite.

Luscious Cakes
& Cheesecakes

Make any day a celebration with these delightful cakes and marvelous cheesecakes. You'll find they are fun to make—and impossible to resist.

Cherry-Topped Lemon Cheesecake Pie

1 (8-ounce) package cream cheese, softened

1 (14-ounce) can EAGLE® BRAND Sweetened Condensed Milk
    (NOT evaporated milk)

$^1/_3$ cup lemon juice from concentrate

1 teaspoon vanilla extract

1 (6-ounce) ready-made graham cracker crumb pie crust

1 (21-ounce) can cherry pie filling, chilled

1. In large mixing bowl, beat cream cheese until fluffy. Gradually beat in Eagle Brand until smooth. Stir in lemon juice and vanilla. Pour into crust. Chill at least 3 hours.

2. To serve, top with cherry pie filling. Store covered in refrigerator.

Makes 6 to 8 servings

Prep Time: 10 minutes
Chill Time: 3 hours

*For a firmer crust, brush crust with slightly beaten
egg white; bake in 375°F oven 5 minutes. Cool
before pouring filling into crust.*

Raspberry Swirl Cheesecakes

1 1/2 cups fresh or thawed lightly sweetened loose-pack frozen red
      raspberries

1 (14-ounce) can EAGLE® BRAND Sweetened Condensed Milk
      (NOT evaporated milk), divided

2 (8-ounce) packages cream cheese, softened

3 eggs

2 (6-ounce) chocolate-flavored crumb pie crusts
      Chocolate and white chocolate leaves (recipe follows), if desired
      Fresh raspberries, if desired

1. Preheat oven to 350°F. In blender container, blend 1 1/2 cups
raspberries until smooth; press through sieve to remove seeds. Stir 1/3 cup
Eagle Brand into sieved raspberries; set aside.

2. In large mixing bowl, beat cream cheese, eggs and remaining Eagle
Brand. Spoon into crusts. Drizzle with raspberry mixture. With table
knife, gently swirl raspberry mixture through cream cheese mixture.

3. Bake 25 minutes or until center is nearly set when shaken. Cool; chill
at least 4 hours. Garnish with chocolate leaves and fresh raspberries, if
desired. Store leftovers covered in refrigerator.

Makes 16 servings (2 cheesecakes)

Prep Time: 15 minutes
Bake Time: 25 minutes
Chill Time: 4 hours

Chocolate Leaves: Place 1 (1-ounce) square semi-sweet or white chocolate in microwave-safe bowl. Microwave at HIGH (100% power) 1 to 2 minutes, stirring every minute until smooth. With small, clean paintbrush, paint several coats of melted chocolate on the undersides of nontoxic leaves, such as mint, lemon or strawberry. Wipe off any chocolate from top sides of leaves. Place leaves, chocolate sides up, on waxed paper-lined baking sheet or on curved surface, such as rolling pin. Refrigerate leaves until chocolate is firm. To use, carefully peel leaves away from chocolate.

Rich Caramel Cake

    1 (14-ounce) package caramels, unwrapped
    ¹/₂ cup (1 stick) butter or margarine
    1 (14-ounce) can EAGLE® BRAND Sweetened Condensed Milk
        (NOT evaporated milk)
    1 (18.25 or 18.5-ounce) package chocolate cake mix
    1 cup coarsely chopped pecans

1. Preheat oven 350°F. In heavy saucepan over low heat, melt caramels and butter. Remove from heat; add Eagle Brand. Mix well. Set aside caramel mixture. Prepare cake mix as package directs.

2. Spread 2 cups cake batter into greased 13×9-inch baking pan; bake 15 minutes. Spread caramel mixture evenly over cake; spread remaining cake batter over caramel mixture. Top with pecans. Return to oven; bake 30 to 35 minutes or until cake springs back when lightly touched. Cool.

Makes 10 to 12 servings

Triple Chocolate Cheesecakes

    1 envelope unflavored gelatin
 1/2 cup cold water
    2 (8-ounce) packages cream cheese, softened
    1 (14-ounce) can EAGLE® BRAND Sweetened Condensed Milk
        (NOT evaporated milk)
    4 (1-ounce) squares unsweetened chocolate, melted and slightly
        cooled
    1 (8-ounce) carton frozen non-dairy whipped topping, thawed
 1/2 cup (3 ounces) mini semi-sweet chocolate chips
    1 (21-ounce) can cherry pie filling, if desired
    2 (6-ounce) ready-made chocolate crumb pie crusts

1. In 1-cup glass measure, stir together gelatin and cold water; let stand 5 minutes to soften. Pour about 1 inch water into small saucepan; place glass measure in saucepan. Place saucepan over medium heat; stir until gelatin is dissolved. Remove measure from saucepan; cool slightly.

2. In large mixing bowl, combine cream cheese, Eagle Brand and melted chocolate; beat until smooth. Gradually beat in gelatin mixture. Fold in whipped topping and chips.

3. Spread pie filling on bottoms of crusts, if desired. Spoon chocolate mixture into pie crusts. Cover and chill at least 4 hours. Store covered in refrigerator.   *Makes 12 servings (2 cheesecakes)*

Prep Time: 20 minutes
Chill Time: 4 hours

Triple Chocolate Cheesecake

Black Forest Chocolate Cheesecake

1 1/2 cups chocolate cookie or wafer crumbs

3 tablespoons butter or margarine, melted

2 (1-ounce) squares unsweetened chocolate

1 (14-ounce) can EAGLE® BRAND Sweetened Condensed Milk
(NOT evaporated milk)

2 (8-ounce) packages cream cheese, softened

3 eggs

3 tablespoons cornstarch

1 teaspoon almond extract

1 (21-ounce) can cherry pie filling, chilled

1. Preheat oven to 300°F. Combine cookie crumbs with butter; press firmly on bottom of 9-inch springform pan.

2. In small saucepan over low heat, melt chocolate with Eagle Brand, stirring constantly. Remove from heat.

3. In large mixing bowl, beat cream cheese until fluffy. Gradually add Eagle Brand mixture until smooth. Add eggs, cornstarch and almond extract; mix well. Pour into crust.

4. Bake 55 minutes or until center is almost set. Cool. Chill. Top with cherry pie filling before serving. Refrigerate leftovers.

Makes one 9-inch cheesecake

Microwave Cheesecake

$^1/_3$ cup ($^2/_3$ stick) butter or margarine

1$^1/_4$ cups graham cracker crumbs

$^1/_4$ cup sugar

2 (8-ounce) packages cream cheese, softened

1 (14-ounce) can EAGLE® BRAND Sweetened Condensed Milk
(NOT evaporated milk)

3 eggs

$^1/_4$ cup lemon juice from concentrate

1 (8-ounce) container sour cream, at room temperature

1. In 10-inch microwave-safe quiche dish or pie plate, melt butter loosely covered at HIGH (100% power) 1 minute. Add crumbs and sugar; press firmly on bottom of dish. Microwave at HIGH (100% power) 1$^1/_2$ minutes, rotating dish once.

2. In 2-quart glass measure, beat cream cheese until fluffy. Gradually beat in Eagle Brand until smooth. Add eggs and lemon juice; mix well. Microwave at MEDIUM-HIGH (70% power) 6 to 8 minutes or until hot, stirring every 2 minutes.

3. Pour into prepared crust. Microwave at MEDIUM (50% power) 6 to 8 minutes or until center is set, rotating dish once. Top with sour cream. Cool. Chill 3 hours or until set. Serve or top with fruit, if desired. Store covered in refrigerator. *Makes one 10-inch cheesecake*

Prep Time: 15 minutes
Cook Time: 14$^1/_2$ to 18$^1/_2$ minutes
Chill Time: 3 hours

Fudge Ribbon Cake

1 (18.25-ounce) package chocolate cake mix
1 (8-ounce) package cream cheese, softened
2 tablespoons butter or margarine, softened
1 tablespoon cornstarch
1 (14-ounce) can EAGLE® BRAND Sweetened Condensed Milk
    (NOT evaporated milk)
1 egg
1 teaspoon vanilla extract
    Chocolate Glaze (recipe follows)

1. Preheat oven to 350°F. Grease and flour 13×9-inch baking pan. Prepare cake mix as package directs. Pour batter into prepared pan.

2. In small mixing bowl, beat cream cheese, butter and cornstarch until fluffy. Gradually beat in Eagle Brand. Add egg and vanilla; beat until smooth. Spoon evenly over cake batter.

3. Bake 40 minutes or until wooden pick inserted near center comes out clean. Cool. Prepare Chocolate Glaze and drizzle over cake. Store covered in refrigerator.   *Makes 10 to 12 servings*

Prep Time: 20 minutes
Bake Time: 40 minutes

Chocolate Glaze: In small saucepan over low heat, melt 1 (1-ounce) square unsweetened or semi-sweet chocolate and 1 tablespoon butter or margarine with 2 tablespoons water. Remove from heat. Stir in $^3/_4$ cup powdered sugar and $^1/_2$ teaspoon vanilla extract. Stir until smooth and well blended. Makes about $^1/_3$ cup.

Fudge Ribbon Bundt Cake: Preheat oven to 350°F. Grease and flour 10-inch Bundt pan. Prepare cake mix as package directs. Pour batter into prepared pan. Prepare cream cheese topping as directed above; spoon evenly over batter. Bake 50 to 55 minutes or until wooden pick inserted near center comes out clean. Cool 10 minutes. Remove from pan. Cool. Prepare Chocolate Glaze and drizzle over cake. Store covered in refrigerator.

Fudge Ribbon Cake

Lemon Party Cheesecake

1 (18.25- or 18.5-ounce) package yellow cake mix*

4 eggs, divided

$^1/_4$ cup vegetable oil*

2 (8-ounce) packages cream cheese, softened

1 (14-ounce) can EAGLE® BRAND Sweetened Condensed Milk
    (NOT evaporated milk)

$^1/_4$ to $^1/_3$ cup lemon juice from concentrate

2 teaspoons grated lemon peel, if desired

1 teaspoon vanilla extract

*If "pudding added" cake mix is used, decrease oil to 3 tablespoons.

1. Preheat oven to 300°F. Reserve $^1/_2$ cup dry cake mix. In large mixing bowl, combine remaining cake mix, 1 egg and oil; mix well (mixture will be crumbly). Press down firmly on bottom and $1^1/_2$ inches up sides of greased 13×9-inch baking pan.

2. In same bowl, beat cream cheese until fluffy. Gradually beat in Eagle Brand until smooth. Add remaining 3 eggs and reserved $^1/_2$ cup cake mix; beat on medium speed 1 minute. Stir in lemon juice, lemon peel, if desired, and vanilla.

3. Pour into crust. Bake 50 to 55 minutes or until center is set. Cool to room temperature. Chill thoroughly. Cut into squares to serve. Garnish as desired. Refrigerate leftovers.   *Makes 12 to 15 servings*

Prep Time: 20 minutes
Bake Time: 55 minutes

Cool and Minty Party Cake

1 (14-ounce) can EAGLE® BRAND Sweetened Condensed Milk
    (NOT evaporated milk)
2 teaspoons peppermint extract
8 drops green food coloring, if desired
2 cups (1 pint) whipping cream, whipped (do not use non-dairy
    topping)
1 (18.25- or 18.5-ounce) package white cake mix
    Green crème de menthe liqueur
1 (8-ounce) container frozen non-dairy whipped topping, thawed

1. Line 9-inch round layer cake pan with aluminum foil. In large mixing bowl, combine Eagle Brand, peppermint extract and food coloring, if desired. Fold in whipped cream. Pour into prepared pan; cover. Freeze at least 6 hours or until firm.

2. Meanwhile, prepare and bake cake mix as package directs for two 9-inch round layers. Remove from pans; cool completely.

3. With fork, poke holes in cake layers 1-inch apart halfway through each layer. Spoon small amounts of liqueur in holes. Place one cake layer on serving plate; top with ice cream layer, then second cake layer. Trim ice cream layer to edge of cake layers.

4. Frost quickly with whipped topping. Return to freezer at least 6 hours before serving. Garnish as desired. Freeze leftovers.

Makes one 9-inch cake

Creamy Baked Cheesecake

1 ¼ cups graham cracker crumbs

¼ cup sugar

⅓ cup (⅔ stick) butter or margarine, melted

2 (8-ounce) packages cream cheese, softened

1 (14-ounce) can EAGLE® BRAND Sweetened Condensed Milk (NOT evaporated milk)

3 eggs

¼ cup lemon juice from concentrate

1 (8-ounce) container sour cream, at room temperature

Raspberry Topping (recipe follows), if desired

1. Preheat oven to 300°F. In small mixing bowl, combine crumbs, sugar and butter; press firmly on bottom of ungreased 9-inch springform pan.

2. In large mixing bowl, beat cream cheese until fluffy. Gradually beat in Eagle Brand until smooth. Add eggs and lemon juice; mix well. Pour into prepared pan. Bake 50 to 55 minutes or until set.

3. Remove from oven; top with sour cream. Bake 5 minutes longer. Cool. Chill. Prepare Raspberry Topping, if desired, and serve with cheesecake. Store covered in refrigerator.   *Makes one 9-inch cheesecake*

Prep Time: 20 minutes
Bake Time: 55 to 60 minutes
Chill Time: 4 hours

New York Style Cheesecake: Increase cream cheese to 4 (8-ounce) packages and eggs to 4. Proceed as directed, adding 2 tablespoons flour after eggs. Bake 1 hour 10 minutes or until center is set. Omit sour cream. Cool. Chill. Serve and store as directed.

Raspberry Topping

> 1 (10-ounce) package thawed frozen red raspberries in syrup
> 1/4 cup red currant jelly or red raspberry jam
> 1 tablespoon cornstarch

1. Drain 2/3 cup syrup from raspberries.

2. In small saucepan over medium heat, combine syrup, jelly and cornstarch. Cook and stir until slightly thickened and clear. Cool. Stir in raspberries.

Prep Time: 5 minutes

Creamy Baked Cheesecake

Chocolate Sheet Cake

1¼ cups (2½ sticks) butter or margarine, divided

1 cup water

½ cup unsweetened cocoa, divided

2 cups all-purpose flour

1½ cups firmly packed light brown sugar

1 teaspoon baking soda

1 teaspoon ground cinnamon

½ teaspoon salt

1 (14-ounce) can EAGLE® BRAND Sweetened Condensed Milk (NOT evaporated milk), divided

2 eggs

1 teaspoon vanilla extract

1 cup powdered sugar

1 cup coarsely chopped nuts

1. Preheat oven to 350°F. In small saucepan over medium heat, melt 1 cup butter; stir in water and ¼ cup cocoa. Bring to a boil; remove from heat. In large mixing bowl, combine flour, brown sugar, baking soda, cinnamon and salt. Add cocoa mixture; beat well. Stir in ⅓ cup Eagle Brand, eggs and vanilla. Pour into greased 15×10-inch jelly-roll pan. Bake 15 minutes or until cake springs back when lightly touched.

2. In small saucepan over medium heat, melt remaining ¼ cup butter; add remaining ¼ cup cocoa and remaining Eagle Brand. Stir in powdered sugar and nuts. Spread on warm cake.   *Makes one 15×10-inch cake*

Mini Cheesecakes

1 1/2 cups graham cracker or chocolate wafer crumbs

1/4 cup sugar

1/4 cup (1/2 stick) butter or margarine, melted

3 (8-ounce) packages cream cheese, softened

1 (14-ounce) can EAGLE® BRAND Sweetened Condensed Milk
(NOT evaporated milk)

3 eggs

2 teaspoons vanilla extract

1. Preheat oven to 300°F. Combine crumbs, sugar and butter; press equal portions onto bottoms of 24 lightly greased or paper-lined muffin cups.

2. In large mixing bowl, beat cream cheese until fluffy. Gradually beat in Eagle Brand until smooth. Add eggs and vanilla; mix well. Spoon equal amounts of mixture (about 3 tablespoons) into prepared cups. Bake 20 minutes or until cakes spring back when lightly touched. Cool.* Chill. Garnish as desired. Refrigerate leftovers.

Makes about 2 dozen mini cheesecakes

If greased muffin cups are used, cool baked cheesecakes. Freeze 15 minutes; remove with narrow spatula. Proceed as directed above.

Prep Time: 20 minutes
Bake Time: 20 minutes

Chocolate Mini Cheesecakes: Melt 1 cup (6 ounces) semi-sweet chocolate chips; mix into batter. Proceed as directed above, baking 20 to 25 minutes.

German Chocolate Cake

1 (18.25-ounce) package chocolate cake mix

1 cup water

3 eggs

$^1/_2$ cup vegetable oil

1 (14-ounce) can EAGLE® BRAND Sweetened Condensed Milk
   (NOT evaporated milk), divided

3 tablespoons butter or margarine

1 egg yolk

$^1/_3$ cup flaked coconut

$^1/_3$ cup chopped pecans

1 teaspoon vanilla extract

1. Preheat oven to 350°F. Grease and flour 13×9-inch baking pan. In large mixing bowl, combine cake mix, water, 3 eggs, oil and $^1/_3$ cup Eagle Brand. Beat at low speed until moistened; beat at high speed 2 minutes.

2. Pour into prepared pan. Bake 40 to 45 minutes or until wooden pick inserted near center comes out clean.

3. In small saucepan over medium heat, combine remaining Eagle Brand, butter and egg yolk. Cook and stir until thickened, about 6 minutes. Add coconut, pecans and vanilla; spread over warm cake. Store covered in refrigerator. *Makes 10 to 12 servings*

Prep Time: 15 minutes
Bake Time: 40 to 45 minutes

German Chocolate Cake

Frozen Mocha Cheesecake

1 1/4 cups chocolate wafer cookie crumbs (about 24 wafers)

1/4 cup sugar

1/4 cup butter or margarine, melted

1 (8-ounce) package cream cheese, softened

1 (14-ounce) can EAGLE® BRAND Sweetened Condensed Milk (NOT evaporated milk)

2/3 cup chocolate-flavored syrup

1 to 2 tablespoons instant coffee

1 teaspoon hot water

1 cup (1/2 pint) whipping cream, whipped

Additional chocolate crumbs, if desired

1. In medium mixing bowl, combine crumbs, sugar and butter; press firmly on bottom and up side of 8- or 9-inch springform pan or 13×9-inch baking pan.

2. In large mixing bowl, beat cream cheese until fluffy. Gradually beat in Eagle Brand and chocolate syrup until smooth.

3. In small mixing bowl, dissolve coffee in water; add to cream cheese mixture. Mix well. Fold in whipped cream. Pour into crust; cover. Freeze 6 hours or overnight. Garnish with chocolate crumbs, if desired. Store leftovers in freezer.

Makes one 8- or 9-inch cheesecake

Chocolate Chip Cheesecake

1½ cups finely crushed crème-filled chocolate sandwich cookie
     crumbs (about 18 cookies)

2 to 3 tablespoons butter or margarine, melted

3 (8-ounce) packages cream cheese, softened

1 (14-ounce) can EAGLE® BRAND Sweetened Condensed Milk
     (NOT evaporated milk)

3 eggs

2 teaspoons vanilla extract

1 cup mini semi-sweet chocolate chips, divided

1 teaspoon all-purpose flour

1. Preheat oven to 300°F. In small mixing bowl, combine cookie crumbs and butter; press firmly on bottom of 9-inch springform pan.

2. In large mixing bowl, beat cream cheese until fluffy. Gradually beat in Eagle Brand until smooth. Add eggs and vanilla; mix well.

3. In small bowl, toss ½ cup chips with flour to coat; stir into cheese mixture. Pour into crust. Sprinkle remaining ½ cup chips evenly over top.

4. Bake 1 hour or until cake springs back when lightly touched. Cool to room temperature. Chill thoroughly. Garnish as desired. Refrigerate leftovers.

Makes one 9-inch cheesecake

Helpful Hint: For best distribution of chips throughout cheesecake, do not oversoften or overbeat cream cheese.

Holiday Cheese Tarts

1 (8-ounce) package cream cheese, softened
1 (14-ounce) can EAGLE® BRAND Sweetened Condensed Milk
   (NOT evaporated milk)
1/3 cup lemon juice from concentrate
1 teaspoon vanilla extract
2 (4-ounce) packages single serve graham cracker crumb pie crusts
   Assorted fruit (strawberries, blueberries, bananas, raspberries,
      orange segments, cherries, kiwi fruit, grapes, pineapple, etc.)
1/4 cup apple jelly, melted, if desired

1. In medium mixing bowl, beat cream cheese until fluffy. Gradually beat in Eagle Brand until smooth. Stir in lemon juice and vanilla.

2. Spoon into crusts. Chill 2 hours or until set. Just before serving, top with fruit; brush with jelly, if desired. Refrigerate leftovers.

Makes 12 tarts

Prep Time: 10 minutes
Chill Time: 2 hours

Holiday Cheese Tarts

Chocolate Almond Torte

4 eggs, separated
1/2 cup (1 stick) butter or margarine, softened
1 cup sugar
1 teaspoon almond extract
1 teaspoon vanilla extract
1 cup finely chopped toasted almonds
3/4 cup all-purpose flour
1/2 cup unsweetened cocoa
1/2 teaspoon baking powder
1/2 teaspoon baking soda
2/3 cup milk
Chocolate Almond Frosting (recipe follows)

1. Line 2 (8- or 9-inch) round cake pans with waxed paper. Preheat oven to 350°F. In small mixing bowl, beat egg whites until soft peaks form; set aside.

2. In large mixing bowl, beat butter and sugar until fluffy. Add egg yolks and extracts; mix well.

3. In medium mixing bowl, combine almonds, flour, cocoa, baking powder and baking soda; add alternately with milk to butter mixture, beating well after each addition.

4. Fold in beaten egg whites. Pour into prepared pans. Bake 18 to 20 minutes or until wooden pick inserted near centers comes out clean. Cool 10 minutes; remove from pans. Cool completely.

5. Prepare Chocolate Almond Frosting. Split each cake layer; fill and frost with frosting. Store covered in refrigerator.

Makes one 4-layer cake

Prep Time: 30 minutes
Bake Time: 18 to 20 minutes

Chocolate Almond Frosting

2 (1-ounce) squares semi-sweet chocolate, chopped
1 (14-ounce) can EAGLE® BRAND Sweetened Condensed Milk
   (NOT evaporated milk)
1 teaspoon almond extract

1. In heavy saucepan over medium heat, melt chocolate with Eagle Brand. Cook and stir until mixture thickens, about 10 minutes.

2. Remove from heat; cool 10 minutes. Stir in almond extract; cool.

Makes about 1½ cups

Prep Time: 20 minutes

Glorious Pies

Impress family and friends with these decadent chocolate and creamy smooth pies—spectacular desserts that are perfect for any occasion.

Heavenly Chocolate Mousse Pie

    4 (1-ounce) squares unsweetened chocolate, melted
    1 (14-ounce) can EAGLE® BRAND Sweetened Condensed Milk
        (NOT evaporated milk)
1 $\frac{1}{2}$ teaspoons vanilla extract
    1 cup ($\frac{1}{2}$ pint) whipping cream, whipped
    1 (6-ounce) chocolate-flavored crumb pie crust

1. In large mixing bowl, beat chocolate with Eagle Brand and vanilla until well blended.

2. Chill 15 minutes until cooled; stir until smooth. Fold in whipped cream.

3. Pour into crust. Chill thoroughly. Garnish as desired. Refrigerate leftovers.
Makes 1 pie

Prep Time: 20 minutes
Chill Time: 15 minutes

Frozen Peanut Butter Pie

    Chocolate Crunch Crust (recipe follows)
1 (8-ounce) package cream cheese, softened
1 (14-ounce) can EAGLE® BRAND Sweetened Condensed Milk
    (NOT evaporated milk)
$^3/_4$ cup peanut butter
2 tablespoons lemon juice from concentrate
1 teaspoon vanilla extract
1 cup ($^1/_2$ pint) whipping cream, whipped
    Chocolate fudge ice cream topping

1. Prepare Chocolate Crunch Crust. In large mixing bowl, beat cream cheese until fluffy; gradually beat in Eagle Brand then peanut butter until smooth. Stir in lemon juice and vanilla.

2. Fold in whipped cream. Turn into prepared crust. Drizzle topping over pie. Freeze 4 hours or until firm. Return leftovers to freezer.

Makes one 9-inch pie

Prep Time: 20 minutes
Freeze Time: 4 hours

Chocolate Crunch Crust: In heavy saucepan over low heat, melt $^1/_3$ cup butter or margarine and 1 (6-ounce) package semi-sweet chocolate chips. Remove from heat; gently stir in $2^1/_2$ cups oven-toasted rice cereal until completely coated. Press on bottom and up side to rim of buttered 9-inch pie plate. Chill 30 minutes.

Frozen Peanut Butter Pie

Traditional Pumpkin Pie

1 (15-ounce) can pumpkin
1 (14-ounce) can EAGLE® BRAND Sweetened Condensed Milk
    (NOT evaporated milk)
2 eggs
1 teaspoon ground cinnamon
$^1/_2$ teaspoon ground ginger
$^1/_2$ teaspoon ground nutmeg
$^1/_2$ teaspoon salt
1 (9-inch) unbaked pastry shell
    Favorite Topping (recipes follow), if desired

1. Preheat oven to 425°F. In large mixing bowl, combine all ingredients except pastry shell and Favorite Topping; mix well.

2. Pour into prepared pastry shell. Bake 15 minutes.

3. Reduce oven temperature to 350°F. Continue baking 35 to 40 minutes, or as directed with one Favorite Topping, if desired, or until knife inserted 1 inch from edge comes out clean. Cool. Garnish as desired. Store covered in refrigerator.   *Makes one 9-inch pie*

Prep Time: 20 minutes
Bake Time: 50 to 55 minutes

Sour Cream Topping: In medium bowl, combine $1^1/_2$ cups sour cream, 2 tablespoons sugar and 1 teaspoon vanilla extract. After pie has baked 30 minutes at 350°F, spread evenly over top; bake 10 minutes.

Chocolate Glaze: In small saucepan over low heat, melt $1/2$ cup semi-sweet chocolate chips and 1 teaspoon solid shortening. Drizzle or spread over top of baked and cooled pie.

Streusel Topping: In medium mixing bowl, combine $1/2$ cup packed brown sugar and $1/2$ cup all-purpose flour; cut in $1/4$ cup ($1/2$ stick) cold butter or margarine until crumbly. Stir in $1/4$ cup chopped nuts. After pie has baked 30 minutes at 350°F, sprinkle evenly over top; bake 10 minutes.

Lemon Cloud Pie

    1 (14-ounce) can EAGLE® BRAND Sweetened Condensed Milk
       (NOT evaporated milk)
$1/2$ cup lemon juice from concentrate
    Yellow food coloring, if desired
    1 cup whipping cream, whipped
    1 (9-inch) baked pastry shell or graham cracker crumb crust

1. In medium mixing bowl, stir together Eagle Brand, lemon juice and food coloring, if desired. Fold in whipped cream. Pour mixture into baked pastry shell.

2. Chill 3 hours or until set. Garnish as desired. Refrigerate leftovers.

Makes one 9-inch pie

Decadent Brownie Pie

1 (9-inch) unbaked pastry shell
1 cup (6 ounces) semi-sweet chocolate chips
1/4 cup (1/2 stick) butter or margarine
1 (14-ounce) can EAGLE® BRAND Sweetened Condensed Milk
   (NOT evaporated milk)
1/2 cup biscuit baking mix
2 eggs
1 teaspoon vanilla extract
1 cup chopped nuts
   Vanilla ice cream

1. Preheat oven to 375°F. Bake pastry shell 10 minutes; remove from oven. Reduce oven temperature to 325°F.

2. In saucepan over low heat, melt chips with butter.

3. In large mixing bowl, beat chocolate mixture with Eagle Brand, biscuit mix, eggs and vanilla until smooth. Add nuts. Pour into pastry shell.

4. Bake 35 to 40 minutes or until center is set. Serve warm or at room temperature with ice cream. Refrigerate leftovers.   *Makes one 9-inch pie*

Prep Time: 25 minutes
Bake Time: 45 to 50 minutes

Decadent Brownie Pie

Sweet Potato Pecan Pie

1 pound sweet potatoes or yams, cooked and peeled

¼ cup (½ stick) butter or margarine, softened

1 (14-ounce) can EAGLE® BRAND Sweetened Condensed Milk (NOT evaporated milk)

1 teaspoon *each* ground cinnamon, grated orange peel and vanilla extract

½ teaspoon ground nutmeg

¼ teaspoon salt

1 egg

1 (6-ounce) graham cracker crumb pie crust

Pecan Topping (recipe follows)

1. Preheat oven to 425°F. In large mixing bowl, beat hot sweet potatoes and butter until smooth. Add Eagle Brand and remaining ingredients except crust and Pecan Topping; mix well. Pour into crust.

2. Bake 20 minutes. Meanwhile, prepare Pecan Topping.

3. Remove pie from oven; reduce oven temperature to 350°F. Spoon Pecan Topping on pie.

4. Bake 25 minutes longer or until set. Cool. Serve warm or at room temperature. Garnish with orange zest twist, if desired. Refrigerate leftovers.

Makes 1 pie

Pecan Topping: In small mixing bowl, beat together 1 egg and 2 tablespoons dark corn syrup, 2 tablespoons firmly packed brown sugar, 1 tablespoon melted butter and ½ teaspoon maple flavoring. Stir in 1 cup chopped pecans.

Prep Time: 30 minutes
Bake Time: 45 minutes

Sweet Potato Pecan Pie

Chocolate-Peanut Butter Mousse Pie

1 cup chocolate graham cracker crumbs
1/3 cup honey-roasted peanuts, finely chopped
6 tablespoons butter or margarine, softened
1 1/2 cups whipping cream, divided
1 (14-ounce) can EAGLE® BRAND Sweetened Condensed Milk
(NOT evaporated milk), divided
1 1/2 cups semi-sweet chocolate chips
2 (3-ounce) packages cream cheese, softened
3/4 cup creamy peanut butter

1. In medium mixing bowl, combine crumbs, peanuts and butter; press mixture in bottom and up side of 9-inch pie plate. Set aside.

2. Pour 1/2 cup whipping cream into microwave-safe bowl; microwave at HIGH (100% power) 2 minutes. Stir in 1/2 cup Eagle Brand and chips until smooth. Spoon mixture into prepared crust. Chill 1 hour.

3. In large mixing bowl, beat remaining 1 cup whipping cream until stiff peaks form; set aside. In small mixing bowl, beat remaining Eagle Brand, cream cheese and peanut butter until smooth. Fold in 1/3 of whipped cream; fold in remaining whipped cream. Spoon over chocolate filling. Chill 1 hour. Store covered in refrigerator.   *Make one 9-inch pie*

Prep Time: 20 minutes
Chill Time: 2 hours

Creamy Lemon Meringue Pie

3 eggs, separated

1 (14-ounce) can EAGLE® BRAND Sweetened Condensed Milk
(NOT evaporated milk)

$^1/_2$ cup lemon juice from concentrate

Few drops yellow food coloring, if desired

1 (8- or 9-inch) baked pastry shell or graham cracker crumb pie
crust

$^1/_4$ teaspoon cream of tartar

$^1/_3$ cup sugar

1. Preheat oven to 350°F. In medium mixing bowl, beat egg yolks; stir in Eagle Brand, lemon juice and food coloring, if desired. Pour into baked pastry shell.

2. In small mixing bowl, beat egg whites and cream of tartar until soft peaks form; gradually add sugar, beating until stiff but not dry. Spread meringue on top of pie, sealing carefully to edge of shell. Bake 12 to 15 minutes or until golden brown. Cool. Chill thoroughly. Refrigerate leftovers. *Makes one 8- or 9-inch pie*

Key Lime Pie

3 eggs, separated

1 (14-ounce) can EAGLE® BRAND Sweetened Condensed Milk
(NOT evaporated milk)

$^{1}/_{2}$ cup lime juice from concentrate

2 to 3 drops green food coloring, if desired

1 (9-inch) unbaked pastry shell

$^{1}/_{2}$ teaspoon cream of tartar

$^{1}/_{3}$ cup sugar

1. Preheat oven to 325°F. In medium mixing bowl, beat egg yolks; gradually beat in Eagle Brand and lime juice. Stir in food coloring, if desired. Pour into pastry shell.

2. Bake 30 minutes. Remove from oven. Increase oven temperature to 350°F.

3. Meanwhile, for meringue, with clean mixer, beat egg whites and cream of tartar to soft peaks. Gradually beat in sugar, 1 tablespoon at a time. Beat 4 minutes or until stiff, glossy peaks form and sugar is dissolved.

4. Immediately spread meringue over hot pie, carefully sealing to edge of crust to prevent meringue from shrinking. Bake 15 minutes. Cool 1 hour. Chill at least 3 hours. Store covered in refrigerator.

Makes one 9-inch pie

Prep Time: 25 minutes
Bake Time: 45 minutes
Cool Time: 1 hour
Chill Time: 3 hours

Key Lime Pie

Fudgy Pecan Pie

$^1/_4$ cup ($^1/_2$ stick) butter or margarine

2 (1-ounce) squares unsweetened chocolate

1 (14-ounce) can EAGLE® BRAND Sweetened Condensed Milk
(NOT evaporated milk)

$^1/_2$ cup hot water

2 eggs, well beaten

1$^1/_4$ cups pecan halves or pieces

1 teaspoon vanilla extract

$^1/_8$ teaspoon salt

1 (9-inch) unbaked pastry shell

1. Preheat oven to 350°F. In medium saucepan over low heat, melt butter and chocolate. Stir in Eagle Brand, hot water and eggs; mix well. Remove from heat; stir in pecans, vanilla and salt.

2. Pour into pastry shell. Bake 40 to 45 minutes or until center is set. Cool slightly. Serve warm or chilled. Garnish as desired. Store covered in refrigerator. *Makes one 9-inch pie*

Prep Time: 15 minutes
Bake Time: 40 to 45 minutes

Fudgy Pecan Pie

Chocolate Chiffon Pie

2 (1-ounce) squares unsweetened chocolate, chopped
1 (14-ounce) can EAGLE® BRAND Sweetened Condensed Milk
(NOT evaporated milk)
1 envelope unflavored gelatin
$^1/_3$ cup water
$^1/_2$ teaspoon vanilla extract
1 cup ($^1/_2$ pint) whipping cream, whipped
1 (6-ounce) ready-made chocolate or graham cracker crumb pie
crust
Additional whipped cream

1. In heavy saucepan over low heat, melt chocolate with Eagle Brand. Remove from heat.

2. Meanwhile, in small saucepan, sprinkle gelatin over water; let stand 1 minute. Over low heat, stir until gelatin dissolves.

3. Stir gelatin into chocolate mixture. Add vanilla. Cool to room temperature. Fold in whipped cream. Spread into crust.

4. Chill 3 hours or until set. Garnish with additional whipped cream. Store covered in refrigerator. *Makes 1 pie*

Prep Time: 20 minutes
Chill Time: 3 hours

Chocolate Chiffon Pie

Lemon Icebox Pie

1 1/2 cups vanilla wafer crumbs (about 40 wafers)
  1/4 cup (1/2 stick) butter or margarine, melted
   1 envelope unflavored gelatin
1 3/4 cups water, divided
   1 (14-ounce) can EAGLE® BRAND Sweetened Condensed Milk
     (NOT evaporated milk)
   1 (3-ounce) package *or* 6 tablespoons pre-sweetened lemonade-
     flavor drink crystals

1. In small mixing bowl, combine crumbs and butter; press firmly on bottom and up side of 9-inch pie plate. Chill.

2. Meanwhile, in small saucepan, sprinkle gelatin over 1/4 cup water; let stand 1 minute. Over low heat, stir until gelatin dissolves; set aside.

3. In medium mixing bowl, combine Eagle Brand, remaining 1 1/2 cups water and lemonade crystals; mix well. Stir in gelatin mixture. Pour into crust.

4. Chill at least 3 hours or until set. Garnish as desired. Refrigerate leftovers. *Makes one 9-inch pie*

Lemon Icebox Pie

Creamy Candy & Desserts

Celebrate with foolproof fudge, melt-in-your-mouth confections, rich ice creams and smooth creamy puddings—irresistible sweets that everyone will enjoy!

Raspberry Almond Trifles

2 cups whipping cream

$^1/_4$ cup plus 1 tablespoon raspberry liqueur or orange juice, divided

1 (14-ounce) can EAGLE® BRAND Sweetened Condensed Milk (NOT evaporated milk)

2 (3-ounce) packages ladyfingers, separated

1 cup seedless raspberry jam

$^1/_2$ cup sliced almonds, toasted

1. In large mixing bowl, beat whipping cream and 1 tablespoon liqueur until stiff peaks form. Fold in Eagle Brand; set aside.

2. Layer bottom of 12 (4-ounce) custard cups or ramekins with ladyfingers. Brush with some remaining liqueur. Spread half of jam over ladyfingers. Spread evenly with half of cream mixture; sprinkle with half of almonds. Repeat layers with remaining ladyfingers, liqueur, jam, cream mixture and almonds. Cover and chill 2 hours. Store covered in refrigerator. *Makes 12 servings*

Prep Time: 20 minutes

Chill Time: 2 hours

Crunchy Clusters

1 (12-ounce) package semi-sweet chocolate chips *or* 3 (6-ounce)
    packages butterscotch-flavored chips
1 (14-ounce) can EAGLE® BRAND Sweetened Condensed Milk
    (NOT evaporated milk)
1 (3-ounce) can chow mein noodles *or* 2 cups pretzel sticks,
    broken into $1/2$-inch pieces
1 cup dry-roasted peanuts or whole roasted almonds

1. Line baking sheet with waxed paper. In heavy saucepan over low heat, melt chips with Eagle Brand. Remove from heat.

2. In large mixing bowl, combine noodles and peanuts; stir in chocolate mixture.

3. Drop by tablespoonfuls onto prepared baking sheet; chill 2 hours or until firm. Store loosely covered at room temperature.

Makes about 3 dozen clusters

Prep Time: 10 minutes
Chill Time: 2 hours

Microwave Directions: In 2-quart glass measure, combine chips and Eagle Brand. Cook at HIGH (100% power) 3 minutes, stirring after $1^{1}/_{2}$ minutes. Stir until smooth. Proceed as directed above.

Clockwise from top: Crunchy Clusters, Peanut Blossom Cookies (page 40) and Easy Peanut Butter Cookies (page 48)

Chocolate Raspberry Truffles

1 (14-ounce) can EAGLE® BRAND Sweetened Condensed Milk
    (NOT evaporated milk)
1/4 cup raspberry liqueur
2 tablespoons butter or margarine
2 tablespoons seedless raspberry jam
2 (12-ounce) packages semi-sweet chocolate chips
1/2 cup powdered sugar or ground toasted almonds

1. In large microwave-safe bowl, combine first 4 ingredients. Microwave at HIGH (100% power) 3 minutes.

2. Stir in chips until smooth. Cover and chill 1 hour.

3. Shape mixture into 1-inch balls and roll in powdered sugar or almonds. Store covered at room temperature.   *Makes 4 dozen truffles*

Prep Time: 10 minutes
Cook Time: 3 minutes
Chill Time: 1 hour

Chocolate Cinnamon Bread Pudding

4 cups soft white bread cubes (5 slices)

1/2 cup chopped nuts

3 eggs

1/4 cup unsweetened cocoa

2 teaspoons vanilla extract

1 teaspoon ground cinnamon

1/2 teaspoon salt

2 3/4 cups water

1 (14-ounce) can EAGLE® BRAND Sweetened Condensed Milk (NOT evaporated milk)

2 tablespoons butter or margarine, melted

Cinnamon Cream Sauce (recipe follows)

1. Preheat oven to 350°F. Place bread cubes and nuts in buttered 9-inch square baking pan. In large mixing bowl, beat eggs, cocoa, vanilla, cinnamon and salt. Add water, Eagle Brand and butter; mix well. Pour evenly over bread, moistening completely.

2. Bake 40 to 45 minutes or until knife inserted into center comes out clean. Cool slightly. Serve warm topped with Cinnamon Cream Sauce. Refrigerate leftovers. *Makes 6 to 9 servings*

Cinnamon Cream Sauce: In medium saucepan over medium-high heat, combine 1 cup whipping cream, 2/3 cup firmly packed light brown sugar, 1 teaspoon vanilla extract and 1/2 teaspoon cinnamon. Bring to a boil; reduce heat and boil rapidly 6 to 8 minutes or until thickened, stirring occasionally. Serve warm.

Foolproof Dark Chocolate Fudge

3 cups (18 ounces) semi-sweet chocolate chips
1 (14-ounce) can EAGLE® BRAND Sweetened Condensed Milk
  (NOT evaporated milk)
Dash salt
1/2 to 1 cup chopped nuts, if desired
2 teaspoons vanilla extract

1. Line 8- or 9-inch square pan with foil. Butter foil; set aside.

2. In heavy saucepan over low heat, melt chips with Eagle Brand and salt.
Remove from heat; stir in nuts, if desired, and vanilla. Spread evenly in
prepared pan.

3. Chill 2 hours or until firm. Turn fudge onto cutting board; peel off foil
and cut into squares. Store covered in refrigerator.

Makes about 2 pounds

Prep Time: 10 minutes
Chill Time: 2 hours

Marshmallow Fudge: Stir in 2 tablespoons butter with vanilla. Substitute
2 cups miniature marshmallows for nuts. Proceed as directed above.

Left to right: Foolproof Dark Chocolate Fudge and Creamy Hot Chocolate (page 121)

Peanut Butter Fudge

2 (10-ounce) packages peanut butter-flavored chips
1 (14-ounce) can EAGLE® BRAND Sweetened Condensed Milk
(NOT evaporated milk)
1/4 cup (1/2 stick) butter or margarine, cut into pieces
1 cup chopped salted peanuts

1. Butter 8-inch square dish. In 2-quart microwave-safe bowl, combine chips, Eagle Brand and butter. Microwave at MEDIUM (50% power) 4 to 5 minutes, stirring at 1 1/2 minute intervals.

2. Stir in peanuts and pour into prepared dish. Cover and chill 2 hours. Cut into squares. Store covered in refrigerator.   *Makes 2 pounds*

Easy Homemade Chocolate Ice Cream

1 (14-ounce) can EAGLE® BRAND Sweetened Condensed Milk
(NOT evaporated milk)
2/3 cup chocolate-flavored syrup
2 cups (1 pint) whipping cream, whipped (DO NOT use
non-dairy whipped topping)

1. In large mixing bowl, combine Eagle Brand and chocolate syrup. Fold in whipped cream. Pour into 9×5-inch loaf pan or other 2-quart container; cover.

2. Freeze 6 hours or until firm. Return leftovers to freezer.
Makes about 1 1/2 quarts ice cream

Rocky Road Candy

1 (12-ounce) package semi-sweet chocolate chips
2 tablespoons butter or margarine
1 (14-ounce) can EAGLE® BRAND Sweetened Condensed Milk
    (NOT evaporated milk)
2 cups dry roasted peanuts
1 (10$^{1}/_{2}$-ounce) package miniature marshmallows

1. Line 13×9-inch baking pan with waxed paper. In heavy saucepan over low heat, melt chips and butter with Eagle Brand; remove from heat.

2. In large mixing bowl, combine peanuts and marshmallows; stir in chocolate mixture. Spread in prepared pan. Chill 2 hours or until firm.

3. Remove candy from pan; peel off paper and cut into squares. Store loosely covered at room temperature.   *Makes about 3$^{1}/_{2}$ dozen candies*

Prep Time: 10 minutes
Chill Time: 2 hours

Microwave Directions: In 1-quart glass measure, combine chips, butter and Eagle Brand. Microwave on HIGH (100% power) 3 minutes, stirring after 1$^{1}/_{2}$ minutes. Stir to melt chips. Let stand 5 minutes. Proceed as directed in Step 2.

Hot Fudge Sauce

1 (6-ounce) package semi-sweet chocolate chips (1 cup) *or*
    4 (1-ounce) squares semi-sweet chocolate
2 tablespoons butter or margarine
1 (14-ounce) can EAGLE® BRAND Sweetened Condensed Milk
    (NOT evaporated milk)
2 tablespoons water
1 teaspoon vanilla extract

1. In heavy saucepan over medium heat, melt chips and butter with Eagle Brand and water. Cook and stir constantly until smooth. Stir in vanilla.

2. Serve warm over ice cream or as dipping sauce for fruit. Refrigerate leftovers. *Makes 2 cups*

Microwave Directions: In 1-quart glass measure, combine ingredients. Microwave at HIGH (100% power) 3 to $3^{1}/_{2}$ minutes, stirring after each minute. Proceed as directed above.

To Reheat: In small heavy saucepan, combine desired amount of Hot Fudge Sauce with small amount of water. Over low heat, stir constantly until heated through.

Spirited Hot Fudge Sauce: Add $^{1}/_{4}$ cup almond, coffee, mint or orange-flavored liqueur with vanilla.

Hot Fudge Sauce

Creamy Caramel Flan

$3/4$ cup sugar

4 eggs

$1^3/4$ cups water

1 (14-ounce) can EAGLE® BRAND Sweetened Condensed Milk (NOT evaporated milk)

$1/2$ teaspoon vanilla extract

$1/8$ teaspoon salt

Sugar Garnish (recipe follows), if desired

1. Preheat oven to 350°F. In heavy skillet over medium heat, cook and stir sugar until melted and caramel-colored. Pour into 8 ungreased 6-ounce custard cups, tilting to coat bottoms.

2. In large mixing bowl, beat eggs; stir in water, Eagle Brand, vanilla and salt. Pour into prepared custard cups. Set cups in large shallow pan. Fill pan with 1 inch hot water.

3. Bake 25 minutes or until knife inserted near centers comes out clean. Cool. Chill. To serve, invert flans onto individual serving plates. Top with Sugar Garnish, if desired, or garnish as desired. Store covered in refrigerator.   *Makes 8 servings*

Prep Time: 15 minutes
Bake Time: 25 minutes

Sugar Garnish: Fill medium metal bowl half-full of ice. In medium saucepan, combine 1 cup sugar with $1/4$ cup water. Stir; cover and bring to a boil. Cook over high heat 5 to 6 minutes or until light brown in color. Immediately put pan in ice for 1 minute. Using spoon, carefully drizzle sugar decoratively over foil. Cool. To serve, peel from foil.

Creamy Caramel Flan

Golden Bread Pudding

    4 cups soft white bread cubes (5 slices)
    3 eggs
    1 teaspoon ground cinnamon
    3 cups warm water
    1 (14-ounce) can EAGLE® BRAND Sweetened Condensed Milk
        (NOT evaporated milk)
    2 tablespoons butter or margarine, melted
    2 teaspoons vanilla extract
    $^1/_2$ teaspoon salt
    Butter Rum Sauce (recipe follows)

1. Preheat oven to 350°F. Place bread cubes in buttered 9-inch square baking pan. In large mixing bowl, beat eggs and cinnamon; add remaining ingredients except Butter Rum Sauce. Pour evenly over bread, moistening completely.

2. Bake 45 to 50 minutes or until knife inserted into center comes out clean. Cool. Serve warm with Butter Rum Sauce. Refrigerate leftovers.

Makes 6 to 9 servings

Butter Rum Sauce: In saucepan over medium-high heat, melt $^1/_4$ cup ($^1/_2$ stick) butter or margarine; add $^3/_4$ cup firmly packed light brown sugar and $^1/_2$ cup whipping cream. Boil rapidly 8 to 10 minutes; add 2 tablespoons rum or 1 teaspoon rum flavoring. Serve warm. Makes about 1 cup.

Dulce de Leche

1 (14-ounce) can EAGLE® BRAND Sweetened Condensed Milk
   (NOT evaporated milk)
Assorted dippers, such as cookies, cake, pound cake, angel food
   cake cubes, banana chunks, apple slices and/or strawberries

1. Preheat oven to 425°F. Pour Eagle Brand into 9-inch pie plate. Cover with foil; place in larger shallow baking pan. Pour hot water into larger pan to depth of 1 inch.

2. Bake 1 hour or until thick and caramel-colored. Beat until smooth. Cool 1 hour. Refrigerate until serving time. Serve as dip with assorted dippers. Store covered in refrigerator for up to 1 week.

Makes about 1¹/₄ cups dip

CAUTION: Never heat an unopened can.

Prep Time: 5 minutes
Bake Time: 1 hour
Cool Time: 1 hour

Fudgy Milk Chocolate Fondue

1 (16-ounce) can chocolate-flavored syrup
1 (14-ounce) can EAGLE® BRAND Sweetened Condensed Milk
    (NOT evaporated milk)
    Dash salt
1 1/2 teaspoons vanilla extract
    Assorted dippers: cookies, cake, pound cake cubes, angel food
    cake cubes, banana chunks, apple slices, strawberries, pear
    slices, kiwifruit slices and/or marshmallows

1. In heavy saucepan over medium heat, combine syrup, Eagle Brand and salt. Cook and stir 12 to 15 minutes or until slightly thickened.

2. Remove from heat; stir in vanilla. Serve warm with assorted dippers. Store covered in refrigerator. *Makes about 3 cups*

Microwave Directions: In 1-quart glass measure, combine syrup, Eagle Brand and salt. Microwave at HIGH (100% power) 3 1/2 to 4 minutes, stirring after 2 minutes. Stir in vanilla.

Helpful Hint: Can be served warm or cold over ice cream. Can be made several weeks ahead. Store tightly covered in refrigerator.

Fudgy Milk Chocolate Fondue

Chocolate Truffles

3 cups (18 ounces) semi-sweet chocolate chips
1 (14-ounce) can EAGLE® BRAND Sweetened Condensed Milk
  (NOT evaporated milk)
1 tablespoon vanilla extract
  Coatings: finely chopped toasted nuts, flaked coconut, chocolate
    sprinkles, colored sugar, unsweetened cocoa, powdered sugar
    or colored sprinkles

1. In heavy saucepan over low heat, melt chips with Eagle Brand. Remove from heat; stir in vanilla. Chill 2 hours or until firm. Shape into 1-inch balls; roll in desired coating.

2. Chill 1 hour or until firm. Store covered at room temperature.

Makes about 6 dozen truffles

Prep Time: 10 minutes
Chill Time: 3 hours

Microwave Directions: In 1-quart measure, combine chips and Eagle Brand. Microwave at HIGH (100% power) 3 minutes, stirring after 1 1/2 minutes. Stir until smooth. Proceed as directed above.

Amaretto Truffles: Substitute 3 tablespoons amaretto liqueur and 1/2 teaspoon almond extract for vanilla. Roll in finely chopped toasted almonds.

Orange Truffles: Substitute 3 tablespoons orange-flavored liqueur for vanilla. Roll in finely chopped toasted almonds mixed with finely grated orange peel.

Rum Truffles: Substitute $^1/_4$ cup dark rum for vanilla. Roll in flaked coconut.

Bourbon Truffles: Substitute 3 tablespoons bourbon for vanilla. Roll in finely chopped toasted nuts.

Chocolate Truffles

Cookies 'n' Crème Fudge

3 (6-ounce) packages white chocolate baking squares
1 (14-ounce) can EAGLE® BRAND Sweetened Condensed Milk
(NOT evaporated milk)
⅛ teaspoon salt
2 cups coarsely crushed chocolate crème-filled sandwich cookies
(about 20 cookies)

1. Line 8-inch square baking pan with foil. In heavy saucepan over low heat, melt chocolate with Eagle Brand and salt. Remove from heat. Stir in crushed cookies. Spread evenly in prepared pan. Chill 2 hours or until firm.

2. Turn fudge onto cutting board. Peel off foil; cut into squares. Store tightly covered at room temperature.   *Makes about 2½ pounds*

Prep Time: 10 minutes
Chill Time: 2 hours

Cookies 'n' Crème Fudge

Chocolate Pudding

1 (14-ounce) can EAGLE® BRAND Sweetened Condensed Milk
  (NOT evaporated milk)
2 cups water, divided
$^1/_4$ teaspoon salt
3 (1-ounce) squares unsweetened chocolate
3 tablespoons cornstarch
1 teaspoon vanilla extract

1. In top of double boiler, combine Eagle Brand, $1^1/_2$ cups water and salt. Add chocolate. Cook over hot water; stir until chocolate melts. Gradually stir remaining $^1/_2$ cup water into cornstarch, keeping mixture smooth. Gradually add to milk mixture; stir rapidly. Continue to cook, stirring constantly until thickened. Stir in vanilla.

2. Divide pudding evenly among six individual dessert dishes. Refrigerate.

Makes six $^1/_2$-cup servings

Party Mints

1 (14-ounce) can EAGLE® BRAND Sweetened Condensed Milk
  (NOT evaporated milk)
1 (32-ounce) package powdered sugar
$^1/_2$ teaspoon peppermint extract
  Assorted colored granulated sugar or crystals

1. In medium mixing bowl, beat Eagle Brand and half of powdered sugar until blended. Gradually add remaining powdered sugar and peppermint extract, beating until stiff.

2. Shape mixture into ½-inch balls; roll in desired sugar and place on lightly greased cooling rack. Let stand 8 hours. Store covered at room temperature.   *Makes 2½ pounds*

Prep Time: 30 minutes
Stand Time: 8 hours

Quick Chocolate Mouse

> 1 (14-ounce) can EAGLE® BRAND Sweetened Condensed Milk (NOT evaporated milk)
> 1 (4-serving-size) package instant chocolate pudding and pie filling mix
> 1 cup cold water
> 1 cup (½ pint) whipping cream, whipped

1. In large mixing bowl, beat Eagle Brand, pudding mix and water; chill 5 minutes.

2. Fold in whipped cream. Spoon into serving dishes; chill. Garnish as desired.   *Makes 8 to 10 servings*

Chocolate Peanut Butter Dessert Sauce

2 (1-ounce) squares semi-sweet chocolate, chopped

2 tablespoons creamy peanut butter

1 (14-ounce) can EAGLE® BRAND Sweetened Condensed Milk (NOT evaporated milk)

2 tablespoons milk

1 teaspoon vanilla extract

1. In medium saucepan over medium-low heat, melt chocolate and peanut butter with Eagle Brand and milk, stirring constantly.

2. Remove from heat; stir in vanilla. Cool slightly. Serve warm over ice cream, cake or as fruit dipping sauce. Store covered in refrigerator.

Makes about 1¹/₂ cups

Prep Time: 15 minutes

Chocolate Peanut Butter Dessert Sauce

Classic Rice Pudding

1 (14-ounce) can EAGLE® BRAND Sweetened Condensed Milk
(NOT evaporated milk)
2 egg yolks
1/4 cup water
1/2 teaspoon ground cinnamon
2 cups uncooked long grain rice, cooked
1/2 cup raisins
2 teaspoons vanilla extract
Additional ground cinnamon

1. In large saucepan, combine Eagle Brand, egg yolks, water and cinnamon. Over medium heat, cook and stir 10 to 15 minutes or until mixture thickens slightly.

2. Remove from heat; add cooked rice, raisins and vanilla. Cool. Chill thoroughly. Sprinkle with additional cinnamon. Refrigerate leftovers.

Makes 8 to 10 servings

Creamy Hot Chocolate

1 (14-ounce) can EAGLE® BRAND Sweetened Condensed Milk
(NOT evaporated milk)
$^1/_2$ cup unsweetened cocoa
$1^1/_2$ teaspoons vanilla extract
$^1/_8$ teaspoon salt
$6^1/_2$ cups hot water
Marshmallows, if desired

1. In large saucepan over medium heat, combine Eagle Brand, cocoa, vanilla and salt; mix well.

2. Slowly stir in water. Heat through, stirring occasionally. Do not boil. Top with marshmallows, if desired. Store covered in refrigerator.

Makes about 2 quarts

Microwave Directions: In 2-quart glass measure, combine all ingredients except marshmallows. Microwave at HIGH (100% power) 8 to 10 minutes, stirring every 3 minutes. Top with marshmallows, if desired. Store covered in refrigerator.

Helpful Hint: Hot chocolate can be stored in the refrigerator for up to 5 days. Mix well and reheat before serving.

Creamy Banana Pudding

1 (14-ounce) can EAGLE® BRAND Sweetened Condensed Milk
(NOT evaporated milk)
1 1/2 cups cold water
1 (4-serving-size) package instant vanilla pudding and pie filling
mix
2 cups (1 pint) whipping cream, whipped
36 vanilla wafers
3 medium bananas, sliced and dipped in lemon juice from
concentrate

1. In large mixing bowl, combine Eagle Brand and water. Add pudding mix; beat until well blended. Chill 5 minutes.

2. Fold in whipped cream. Spoon 1 cup pudding mixture into 2 1/2-quart glass serving bowl.

3. Top with one-third each the vanilla wafers, bananas and pudding mixture. Repeat layering twice, ending with pudding mixture. Chill thoroughly. Garnish as desired. Refrigerate leftovers.

Makes 8 to 10 servings

Prep Time: 15 minutes

Amaretto Truffles, 112
Any-Way-You-Like 'em
    Cookies, 48

Black Forest Chocolate
    Cheesecake, 56
Bourbon Truffles, 113
Brownie Mint Sundae
    Squares, 13
Buckeye Cookie Bars, 30
Butter Rum Sauce, 108

Cakes
    Chocolate Almond Torte,
        72
    Chocolate Sheet Cake,
        64
    Cool and Minty Party
        Cake, 61
    Fudge Ribbon Bundt Cake,
        59
    Fudge Ribbon Cake, 58
    German Chocolate Cake,
        66
    Rich Caramel Cake, 52
Candy
    Amaretto Truffles, 112
    Bourbon Truffles, 113
    Chocolate Raspberry
        Truffles, 98
    Chocolate Truffles, 112
    Cookies 'n' Creme Fudge,
        114
    Crunchy Clusters, 96
    Foolproof Dark Chocolate
        Fudge, 100
    Magic Rainbow Cookie
        Bars, 7
    Marshmallow Fudge, 100
    Orange Truffles, 112
    Party Mints, 116
    Peanut Butter Fudge, 102
    Rocky Road Candy, 103
    Rum Truffles, 113
Cheesecakes
    Black Forest Chocolate
        Cheesecake, 56
    Cherry-Topped Lemon

Cheesecake Pie, 51
Cheesecakes (continued)
    Chocolate Chip
        Cheesecake, 69
    Chocolate Mini
        Cheesecakes, 65
    Creamy Baked Cheesecake,
        62
    Frozen Mocha Cheesecake,
        68
    Holiday Cheese Tarts, 70
    Lemon Party Cheesecake,
        60
    Microwave Cheesecake,
        57
    Mini Cheesecakes, 65
    New York Style
        Cheesecake, 62
    Raspberry Swirl
        Cheesecakes, 52
    Triple Chocolate
        Cheesecakes, 54
Cheesecake-Topped Brownies,
    14
Cherries
    Black Forest Chocolate
        Cheesecake, 56
    Cherry-Topped Lemon
        Cheesecake Pie, 51
    Double Chocolate Cherry
        Cookies, 38
    Triple Chocolate
        Cheesecakes, 54
Cherry-Topped Lemon
    Cheesecake Pie, 51
Chewy Almond Squares, 10
Chocolate (see also **Chocolate
    Chips**)
    Black Forest Chocolate
        Cheesecake, 56
    Brownie Mint Sundae
        Squares, 13
    Buckeye Cookie Bars, 30
    Cheesecake-Topped
        Brownies, 14
    Chocolate Almond Torte,
        72
    Chocolate Chiffon Pie, 90

Chocolate (continued)
    Chocolate Cinnamon
        Bread Pudding, 99
    Chocolate Crunch Crust,
        76
    Chocolate Glaze, 58
    Chocolate Leaves, 52
    Chocolate Mini
        Cheesecakes, 65
    Chocolate Peanut Butter
        Chip Cookies, 37
    Chocolate Peanut Butter
        Dessert Sauce, 118
    Chocolate Pudding, 116
    Chocolate Sheet Cake, 64
    Creamy Hot Chocolate,
        121
    Double Chocolate
        Brownies, 31
    Double Chocolate Cookies,
        44
    Easy Homemade Chocolate
        Ice Cream, 102
    Frozen Mocha Cheesecake,
        68
    Fudge Ribbon Bundt Cake,
        59
    Fudge Ribbon Cake, 58
    Fudgy Milk Chocolate
        Fondue, 110
    Fudgy Pecan Pie, 88
    German Chocolate Cake,
        66
    German Chocolate
        Cheesecake Squares, 24
    Heavenly Chocolate
        Mousse Pie, 75
    Macaroon Kisses, 46
    Marbled Cheesecake Bars,
        12
    Mint Chocolate Cookies,
        44
    No-Bake Fudgy Brownies,
        28
    No-Bake Peanutty
        Chocolate Drops, 43
    Peanut Blossom Cookies,
        49

INDEX

Chocolate *(continued)*
  Quick Chocolate Mousse,
    117
  Rich Caramel Cake, 53
  Triple Chocolate
    Cheesecakes, 54
Chocolate Almond Frosting,
  73
Chocolate Almond Torte, 72
Chocolate Chiffon Pie, 90
Chocolate Chip Cheesecake,
  69
Chocolate Chips
  Amaretto Truffles, 112
  Bourbon Truffles, 112
  Chocolate Chip
    Cheesecake, 69
  Chocolate Chip Treasure
    Cookies, 40
  Chocolate Nut Bars, 16
  Chocolate-Peanut Butter
    Mousse Pie, 84
  Chocolate Raspberry
    Truffles, 98
  Chocolate Truffles, 112
  Crunchy Clusters, 96
  Decadent Brownie Pie,
    80
  Double Chocolate Cherry
    Cookies, 38
  Double Chocolate Fantasy
    Bars, 8
  Double Chocolate Pecan
    Cookies, 39
  Double Delicious Cookie
    Bars, 32
  Foolproof Dark Chocolate
    Fudge, 100
  Fudge-Filled Bars, 26
  Hot Fudge Sauce, 104
  Magic Cookie Bars, 7
  Marshmallow Fudge, 100
  Orange Truffles, 112
  Rocky Road Candy, 103
  Rum Truffles, 112
  Toffee Bars, 19
Chocolate Chip Treasure
  Cookies, 40

Chocolate Cinnamon Bread
  Pudding, 99
Chocolate Crunch Crust, 76
Chocolate Glaze, 58, 79
Chocolate Leaves, 52
Chocolate Mini Cheesecakes,
  65
Chocolate Nut Bars, 16
Chocolate Peanut Butter Chip
  Cookies, 37
Chocolate Peanut Butter
  Dessert Sauce, 118
Chocolate-Peanut Butter
  Mousse Pie, 84
Chocolate Pudding, 116
Chocolate Raspberry Truffles,
  98
Chocolate Sheet Cake, 64
Chocolate Truffles, 112
Cinnamon Cream Sauce, 99
Classic Rice Pudding, 120
Coconut
  Chewy Almond Squares,
    10
  Chocolate Chip Treasure
    Cookies, 40
  Coconut Macaroons, 39
  Coconut Pecan Topping,
    24
  Macaroon Kisses, 46
  Magic Cookie Bars, 7
  7-Layer Magic Cookie
    Bars, 7
Coconut Macaroons, 39
Coconut Pecan Topping, 24
Cookies 'n' Crème Fudge,
  114
Cool and Minty Party Cake,
  61
Creamy Baked Cheesecake,
  62
Creamy Banana Pudding,
  122
Creamy Caramel Flan, 106
Creamy Hot Chocolate, 121
Creamy Lemon Meringue Pie,
  85
Crunchy Clusters, 96

Decadent Brownie Pie, 80
Desserts
  Chocolate Cinnamon
    Bread Pudding, 99
  Chocolate Pudding, 116
  Classic Rice Pudding,
    120
  Creamy Banana Pudding,
    122
  Creamy Caramel Flan,
    106
  Easy Homemade Chocolate
    Ice Cream, 102
  Fudgy Milk Chocolate
    Fondue, 110
  Golden Bread Pudding,
    108
  Raspberry Almond Trifles,
    95
Double Chocolate Brownies,
  31
Double Chocolate Cherry
  Cookies, 38
Double Chocolate Cookies,
  44
Double Chocolate Fantasy
  Bars, 8
Double Chocolate Pecan
  Cookies, 39
Double Delicious Cookie
  Bars, 32
Dulce de Leche, 109

Easy Homemade Chocolate
  Ice Cream, 102
Easy Peanut Butter Cookies,
  48

Foolproof Dark Chocolate
  Fudge, 100
Frozen Lemon Squares, 25
Frozen Mocha Cheesecake,
  68
Frozen Peanut Butter Pie, 76
Fudge-Filled Bars, 26
Fudge Ribbon Bundt Cake,
  59
Fudge Ribbon Cake, 58

Fudgy Milk Chocolate Fondue, 110
Fudgy Pecan Pie, 88

German Chocolate Cake, 66
German Chocolate Cheesecake Squares, 24
Golden Bread Pudding, 108
Golden Peanut Butter Bars, 34

Heavenly Chocolate Mousse Pie, 75
Holiday Cheese Tarts, 70
Hot Fudge Sauce, 104

Key Lime Pie, 86

Lemon
    Cherry-Topped Lemon Cheesecake Pie, 51
    Creamy Lemon Meringue Pie, 85
    Frozen Lemon Squares, 25
    Lemon Cloud Pie, 79
    Lemon Crumb Bars, 20
    Lemon Icebox Pie, 92
    Lemon Party Cheesecake, 60
    Lemony Cheesecake Bars, 18
Lemon Cloud Pie, 79
Lemon Crumb Bars, 20
Lemon Icebox Pie, 92
Lemon Party Cheesecake, 60
Lemony Cheesecake Bars, 18

Macaroon Kisses, 46
Magic Cookie Bars, 7
Magic Make It Your Way Drop Cookies, 42
Magic Peanut Cookie Bars, 7
Magic Rainbow Cookie Bars, 7
Marbled Cheesecake Bars, 12
Marshmallow Fudge, 100
Microwave Cheesecake, 57
Mini Cheesecakes, 65
Mint Chocolate Cookies, 44

New York Style Cheesecake, 62
No-Bake Fudgy Brownies, 28
No-Bake Peanutty Chocolate Drops, 43
Nuts (see also **Peanuts**; **Pecans**)
    Chocolate Chip Treasure Cookies, 40
    Chocolate Nut Bars, 16
    Chocolate Sheet Cake, 64
    Decadent Brownie Pie, 80
    Double Chocolate Fantasy Bars, 8
    Foolproof Dark Chocolate Fudge, 100
    Magic Cookie Bars, 7
    Magic Rainbow Cookie Bars, 7
    Raspberry Almond Trifles, 95
    7-Layer Magic Cookie Bars, 7

Orange Truffles, 112

Party Mints, 116
Peanut Blossom Cookies, 49
Peanut Butter
    Chocolate Peanut Butter Dessert Sauce, 118
    Chocolate-Peanut Butter Mousse Pie, 84
    Easy Peanut Butter Cookies, 48
    Frozen Peanut Butter Pie, 76
    Golden Peanut Butter Bars, 34
    Peanut Blossom Cookies, 49
    Peanut Butter & Jelly Gems, 48
    Peanut Butter Fudge, 102
Peanuts
    Buckeye Cookie Bars, 30
    Crunchy Clusters, 96
    Golden Peanut Butter Bars, 34

Peanuts (continued)
    Magic Peanut Cookie Bars, 7
    No-Bake Peanutty Chocolate Drops, 43
    Peanut Butter Fudge, 102
    Rocky Road Candy, 103
Pecans
    Coconut Pecan Topping, 24
    Double Chocolate Pecan Cookies, 39
    Fudgy Pecan Pie, 88
    Pecan Topping, 82
    Rich Caramel Cake, 52

Quick Chocolate Mousse, 117

Raspberry
    Chocolate Raspberry Truffles, 98
    Raspberry Almond Trifles, 95
    Raspberry Swirl Cheesecakes, 52
    Raspberry Topping, 63
Raspberry Almond Trifles, 95
Raspberry Swirl Cheesecakes, 52
Raspberry Topping, 63
Rich Caramel Cake, 53
Rocky Road Candy, 103
Rum Truffles, 113

7-Layer Magic Cookie Bars, 7
Sour Cream Topping, 78
Spirited Hot Fudge Sauce, 104
Streusel Topping, 79
Sugar Garnish, 106
Sweet Potato Pecan Pie, 82

Toffee Bars, 19
Toffee-Top Cheesecake Bars, 22
Traditional Pumpkin Pie, 78
Triple Chocolate Cheesecakes, 54

VOLUME MEASUREMENTS (dry)

$1/8$ teaspoon = 0.5 mL
$1/4$ teaspoon = 1 mL
$1/2$ teaspoon = 2 mL
$3/4$ teaspoon = 4 mL
1 teaspoon = 5 mL
1 tablespoon = 15 mL
2 tablespoons = 30 mL
$1/4$ cup = 60 mL
$1/3$ cup = 75 mL
$1/2$ cup = 125 mL
$2/3$ cup = 150 mL
$3/4$ cup = 175 mL
1 cup = 250 mL
2 cups = 1 pint = 500 mL
3 cups = 750 mL
4 cups = 1 quart = 1 L

VOLUME MEASUREMENTS (fluid)

1 fluid ounce (2 tablespoons) = 30 mL
4 fluid ounces ($1/2$ cup) = 125 mL
8 fluid ounces (1 cup) = 250 mL
12 fluid ounces ($1 1/2$ cups) = 375 mL
16 fluid ounces (2 cups) = 500 mL

WEIGHTS (mass)

$1/2$ ounce = 15 g
1 ounce = 30 g
3 ounces = 90 g
4 ounces = 120 g
8 ounces = 225 g
10 ounces = 285 g
12 ounces = 360 g
16 ounces = 1 pound = 450 g

DIMENSIONS

$1/16$ inch = 2 mm
$1/8$ inch = 3 mm
$1/4$ inch = 6 mm
$1/2$ inch = 1.5 cm
$3/4$ inch = 2 cm
1 inch = 2.5 cm

OVEN TEMPERATURES

250°F = 120°C
275°F = 140°C
300°F = 150°C
325°F = 160°C
350°F = 180°C
375°F = 190°C
400°F = 200°C
425°F = 220°C
450°F = 230°C

BAKING PAN SIZES

Utensil	Size in Inches/Quarts	Metric Volume	Size in Centimeters
Baking or Cake Pan (square or rectangular)	8×8×2	2 L	20×20×5
	9×9×2	2.5 L	23×23×5
	12×8×2	3 L	30×20×5
	13×9×2	3.5 L	33×23×5
Loaf Pan	8×4×3	1.5 L	20×10×7
	9×5×3	2 L	23×13×7
Round Layer Cake Pan	8×1½	1.2 L	20×4
	9×1½	1.5 L	23×4
Pie Plate	8×1¼	750 mL	20×3
	9×1¼	1 L	23×3
Baking Dish or Casserole	1 quart	1 L	—
	1½ quart	1.5 L	—
	2 quart	2 L	—